한국어 자습서
Talk To Me In Korean - Level 2

This book is based on a series of published lessons,
divided into ten levels, which are currently available
at TalkToMeInKorean.com.

Talk To Me In Korean - Level 2

First edition published		2012. 11. 05.
Third published		2014. 5. 30.

Written by		TalkToMeInKorean
Edited by		Kyung-hwa Sun
Design by		Yoona Sun, Ji-eun Son
Illustration by		Kyoung-hae Kim
Voice Recording by		Kyeong-eun Choi, Hyunwoo Sun, Seokjin Jin

Published by		Language Plus (Hangulpark)
President		Ho-yeul Eom
Publisher		Tae-sang Eom
Editor in Chief		Yi-jun Kwon
Registration Date		2000. 8. 17.
Registration Number		1-2718
Address		Songmin Building, 300, Jahamun ro, Jongro gu, Seoul
Telephone		
	Inquiry	+82-(0)2-764-1009
	Order	+82-(0)2-3671-0555
Fax		+82-(0)2-3671-0500
Website		http://www.hangulpark.com
E-mail		info@langpl.com
ISBN		978-89-5518-185-2 18710
		978-89-5518-183-8 (set)

Message from the Author

We are very happy to present you with the 2nd Level of the TalkToMeInKorean book series. Whether you already studied with the Level 1 book, or you haven chosen this book because it is the right level for you, we hope that you enjoy learning Korean with us.

When learning a new language, especially if you are studying on your own, it is very important to find ways to improve your listening skills as well as practice speaking, reading, and writing. We strongly recommend that you to use every opportunity you can find to practice what you learn through this book, and please remember that we are always available online at your favorite social media channels to help you practice.

After completion of this book, you will be able to hold simple conversations in Korean. Level 1 and Level 2 introduce the most essential sentence structures and various tenses which give you the foundation you need to take your Korean language skills even further through subsequent lessons and practice.

Thank you once again, everyone, for giving us your support and for studying with TalkToMeInKorean online and now with this book! We hope you continue having fun learning Korean!

Contents

LESSON 01

〜〜〜

-ㄹ/을 거예요

Track 01

Welcome to Level 2 and congratulations on making your way through Level 1!
In Level 2, we will study grammar and expressions to help build upon what you
learned in Level 1.

In this lesson, we are going to learn how to talk about the future in Korean.

Future Tense

The most common way of making future tense sentences in Korean is by adding
ㄹ/을 거예요.
[l/eul geo-ye-yo.]

Verb + ㄹ/을 거예요 = future tense

How to determine whether to use ㄹ 거예요 or 을 거예요:
1. Verb stems ending with a vowel (보다, 가다, 자다) are followed by ㄹ 거예요.
보다 + ㄹ/을 거예요 = 볼 거예요.
가다 + ㄹ/을 거예요 = 갈 거예요.
자다 + ㄹ/을 거예요 = 잘 거예요.

2. Verb stems ending with a consonant (먹다, 찾다, 붙다) are followed by 을 거예요.
먹다 + ㄹ/을 거예요 = 먹을 거예요.
찾다 + ㄹ/을 거예요 = 찾을 거예요.

붙다 + ㄹ/을 거예요 = 붙을 거예요.

(**There is no complex reason for this. It's just for the ease of pronunciation.)

3. Exception: Verb stems already ending with ㄹ at the end (놀다, 멀다, 살다) are followed only by 거예요.

놀다 + ㄹ/을 거예요 = 놀 거예요.

멀다 + ㄹ/을 거예요 = 멀 거예요.

살다 + ㄹ/을 거예요 = 살 거예요.

When a verb is changed into this form, it takes on the meaning of "to be going to" do something or "will" do something, but as you will find out when you hear more conversations between native speakers, the present tense can also serve to express the future, when the context is very clear.

For example, "I'm going to go tomorrow" is "내일 갈 거예요" in the future tense Korean, but even if you say "내일 가요" (which is in the present tense), it still makes perfect sense, depending on the situation.

Sample Sentences

1. 가다 = to go   가 + ㄹ 거예요.
   [ga-da]   [ga + l geo-ye-yo.]
   → 갈 거예요. = I'm going to go. I will go.
     [gal geo-ye-yo.]

   지금 갈 거예요. = I'm going to go (there) now.

   혼자 갈 거예요. = I'm going to go alone.

   내일 갈 거예요. = I'm going to go tomorrow.

2. 하다 = to do   하 + ㄹ 거예요.
   [ha-da]   [ha + l geo-ye-yo.]
   → 할 거예요. = I'm going to do (it). I will do (it).
     [hal geo-ye-yo.]

   뭐 할 거예요? = What are you going to do?

   언제 할 거예요? = When are you going to do (it)?

이거 언제 할 거예요? = When are you going to do this?

이거 정말 할 거예요? = Are you really going to do it?

3. 입다 = to wear   입 + 을 거예요.
   [ip-da]   [ip + eul geo-ye-yo.]
   → 입을 거예요. = I'm going to wear (it). I will wear (it).
     [i-beul geo-ye-yo]

   청바지 입을 거예요. = I'm going to wear blue jeans.

   뭐 입을 거예요? = What are you going to wear?

   티셔츠 입을 거예요. = I'm going to wear a t-shirt.

   치마 입을 거예요. = I'm going to wear a skirt.

4. 만나다 = to meet   만나 + ㄹ 거예요.
   [man-na-da]   [man-na l geo-ye-yo.]
   → 만날 거예요. = I'm going to meet (him/her/that person/them). I will meet (him/
     [man-nal geo-ye-yo.]
   her/that person/them).

   누구 만날 거예요? = Who are you going to meet?

   어디에서 만날 거예요? = Where are you going to meet?

   언제 만날 거예요? = When are you going to meet?

5. 팔다 = to sell   팔 + 거예요.
   [pal-da]   [pal geo-ye-yo.]
   → 팔 거예요. = I'm going to sell (it). I will sell (it).
     [pal geo-ye-yo.]

   뭐 팔 거예요? = What are you going to sell?

   어디에서 팔 거예요? = Where are you going to sell it?

   얼마에 팔 거예요? = At what price are you going to sell it?

Sample dialogue

Track 02

A: 저 여행 갈 거예요.
[jeo yeo-haeng gal geo-ye-yo.]

B: 우와! 어디로 갈 거예요?
[u-wa! eo-di-ro gal geo-ye-yo?]

A: 보라카이로 갈 거예요.
[bo-ra-ka-i-ro gal geo-ye-yo.]

A: I'm going on a trip.
B: Wow! Where are you going to go?
A: I'm going to Boracay.

Exercises for Level 2 Lesson 1

Translates the following sentences into Korean:

1. "I'm going to wear blue jeans."
(입다 = to wear, 청바지 = blue jeans)
[ip-da]   [cheong-ba-ji]

(   )

2. "What are you going to sell?"
(팔다 = to sell)
[pal-da]

(   )

3. "Who are you going to meet?"
(만나다 = to meet)
[man-na-da]

(   )

4. "When are you going to eat lunch?"
(점심 = lunch, 먹다 = to eat)
[jeom-sim]   [meok-da]

(   )

5. "What are you going to do tomorrow?"

(   )

Check the
Answers on
p. 177

LESSON 02

〰〰〰〰

을, 를

Track 03

In this lesson, we are looking at the **object marking particles**. As we have mentioned a few times through our previous lessons, there are different types of particles in Korean, such as subject marking particles, topic marking particles, location marking particles, and so on. These particles are what make Korean sentences easier to understand, even when the word order changes.

More often than not, when the meaning of a certain sentence can be very clear WITHOUT using a certain particle, Korean speakers like to drop the particle and just not say it. Like many other rules in speaking Korean, this is also for the ease of pronunciation and for the shortening of the phrase.

For example, let's look at "친구가 왔어요" and "친구 왔어요". Which one of these easier to pronounce? That's right! "친구 왔어요" is easier to say, and even though "친구가 왔어요" has only one more letter added to it which does not make the sentence too much longer, nor is all that difficult to pronounce, it's just nicer to be able to say less and express the same meaning. That's why a lot of particles are dropped in Korean sentences, especially during conversations.

So far, we have looked at many verbs. Verbs can be divided into transitive verbs (verbs that need an object) and intransitive verbs (verbs that do not need an object).

In English, this is clearer than in Korean because even when a noun is repeatedly referred to (i. e. "Did you find your wallet? / Yes, I found it.), you do not get rid of the part that refers to "the wallet" - you still have it there by saying "it" instead of "the wallet".

However, using the same mini dialogue as above, let's see how it would be said in Korean : "**지갑 찾았어요?**" (literal translation: "wallet found?") / "**네. 찾았어요.**" (literal translation: "yes. found."). As you can see, the distinction between transitive verbs and intransitive verbs in Korean is not as strong as in English and many other languages.

That's where object marking particles come in to play.

Object marking particles:

을 - used after a noun ending in a consonant
를 - used after a noun ending in a vowel

우유(milk) + 를
책(book) + 을 [reul]
모자(hat) + 를 [eul]
카메라(camera) + 를
방(room) + 을

So, what exactly does an object marking particle do?

In English, if you write "an apple" and do not write a verb to go with it, there is no way for you to tell what kind of role the apple is going to take on in the sentence.

But in Korean, even if you do not write or say the verb that goes with "an apple", just by adding the right particle after the noun, you can express the role of the noun or pronoun even before you say the verb.

"An apple" - in English, it's completely neutral as is.

"사과" - in Korean, as is, it's neutral, too.

"사과를" - even if you don't say the verb, you know that 사과 is going to be the OBJECT of the verb.

In Korean, you can predict the verbs to an extent - "eat an apple, buy an apple, sell an apple, find an apple, throw an apple, draw an apple, etc."

" 사과가" - you know that 사과 is going to be the SUBJECT of the verb.
You can predict the verbs here as well - "the apple is good, is bad, is expensive, will be big, was small, can be good for health, etc."

" 사과는" - you know that the speaker is going to say something about 사과 in comparison to other things, or the speaker is bringing up the topic of 사과 for the first time.

How object marking particles are dropped

If you want to directly translate the question "what did you do yesterday?" from English to Korean using all the elements, it ends up being very unnatural in Korean.

= "어제 <the name of the other person> 씨는 뭐를 했어요?"

Unless you are talking about a THIRD person, you don't need to say the name of the other person here. Therefore, it becomes

= "어제 뭐를 했어요?"

Since it's also clear that "뭐" (what) is NOT the subject of the sentence, (it's the PERSON that did WHAT, not the other way around) you can drop 를.

= "어제 뭐 했어요?"

When do you need to use object marking particles?

You need to use them when you want to clarify the relation between the object and the verb. When the object and the verb are close to each other, you can either add or omit the particle since it doesn't make too much of a difference. In contrast, when the object word is far away from the verb, the relation or connection between the words are weakened, so you need the particle to be used to make the meaning clear.

Sample Sentences

만났어요. = I met.
↓
만났어요? = Did you meet?
↓
누구 만났어요? = Who did you meet?
↓
어제 여기에서 누구(를) 만났어요? = Who did you meet here yesterday?
↓
어제 누구를 여기에서 만났어요? = WHO did you meet here yesterday?

텔레비전 봐요. = I watch TV.
↓
텔레비전 봐요? = Do you watch TV?
↓
텔레비전 자주 봐요? = Do you watch TV often?
↓
일주일에 몇 번 텔레비전 봐요? = How many times per week do you watch TV?
↓
텔레비전(을) 일주일에 몇 번 봐요? = How many times a week do you watch TV?

As the object of the sentences (**텔레비전**) gets further and further away from the verb (**봐요**), you need to make the relation of the words clearer by using the object marking particle.

Sample dialogue

Track 04

A: 헤어스타일을 바꾸고 싶어요
[he-eo-seu-ta-i-reul ba-kku-go si-peo-yo.]

B: 어떻게요?
[eo-tteo-ke-yo?]

A: 머리 색깔을 좀 바꾸고 싶어요.
[meo-ri saek-kka-reul jom ba-kku-go si-peo-yo.]

B: 아! 염색을 하고 싶어요?
[a! yeom-sae-geul ha-go si-peo-yo?]

A: I want to change my hair style.

B: How?

A: I want to change my hair color.

B: Oh, you want to dye your hair?

Exercises for Level 2 Lesson 2

을 and 를 are object marking particles in Korean. Do you remember how to decide
[eul]   [reul]
which one is used? Please fill in the blanks with either "을" or "를".

1. 사과 (   )

2. 핸드폰 (   )

3. 공부 (   )

4. 시계 (   )

5. 여행 (   )

Check the
Answers on
p. 177

LESSON 03

그리고, 그래서

Track 05   After two previous lessons that introduced rather heavy topics (future tense and object marking particles), we would like to introduce something very easy to learn yet very useful to know. Like many languages in the world, there are many conjunctions in the Korean language, and in this lesson, we are introducing two of them: 그리고 and 그래서.

그리고

그리고 has the meaning of "and" or "and then", depending on the context. 그리고 is
[geu-ri-go]
used both for linking nouns and phrases, but in colloquial situations, 그리고 is more commonly used for linking phrases.

Ex) (linking nouns)
- 커피, 빵, 그리고 물 = coffee, bread and water
  [keo-pi, ppang, geu-ri-go mul]
- 서울 그리고 부산 = Seoul and Busan
  [seo-ul geu-ri-go bu-san]
- 런던 그리고 파리 = London and Paris
  [leon-deon geu-ri-go pa-ri]
- 미국 그리고 호주 = United States and Australia
  [mi-guk geu-ri-go ho-ju]
- 독일 그리고 필리핀 = Germany and the Philippines
  [do-gil geu-ri-go pil-li-pin]

Ex) (linking phrases)

(1) **친구를 만났어요**.
[chin-gu-reul man-na-sseo-yo.]

- **친구** = friend
- **를** = object marking particle
- **만나다** = to meet
- **만났어요** = past tense of **만나다**

(2) **밥을 먹었어요**.
[ba-beul meo-geo-sseo-yo.]

- **밥** = rice, meal
- **을** = object marking particle
- **먹다** = to eat
- **먹었어요** = past tense of **먹다**

(1) and (2) = **친구를 만났어요** and **밥을 먹었어요**.
= **친구를 만났어요. 그리고 밥을 먹었어요**.

그래서

그래서 has the meaning of "therefore" and "so", and just like in English, you can use
[geu-rae-seo]
this word between two sentences to show a logical relation between the two or
more sentences.

Ex)
(1) **오늘은 비가 왔어요**.
[o-neu-reun bi-ga wa-sseo-yo.]
- **비가 오다** = to rain
- **비가 왔어요** = past tense of **비가 오다**

(2) 집에 있었어요.
[ji-be i-sseo-sseo-yo.]

- 집 = house, home

- 있다 = to be

- 있었어요 = past tense of 있다

(1) + (2) = 오늘은 비가 왔어요. therefore 집에 있었어요.

= 오늘은 비가 왔어요. 그래서 집에 있었어요.

Sample Sentences

1. 김치는 맛있어요. 그리고 한국 음식이에요.
[gim-chi-neun ma-si-sseo-yo. geu-ri-go han-guk eum-si-gi-e-yo.]
= Kimchi is delicious. And it is Korean food.

   - 김치 = Kimchi

   - 맛있다 = to be delicious

   - 한국 음식 = Korean food

2. 저는 학생이에요. 그리고 프랑스어를 공부해요.
[jeo-neun hak-saeng-i-e-yo. geu-ri-go peu-rang-seu-eo-reul gong-bu-hae-yo.]
= I am a student. And I am studying French.

   - 저 = I (humble)

   - 학생 = student

   - 프랑스어 = French (language)

   - 공부하다 = to study

3. 저는 학생이에요. 그래서 돈이 없어요.
[jeo-neun hak-saeng-i-e-yo. geu-rae-seo do-ni eop-sseo-yo.]
= I am a student. So I don't have money.

   - 돈 = money

   - 없다 = to not be, to not exist

4. 김치는 맛있어요. 그래서 김치를 많이 먹어요.
[gim-chi-neun ma-si-sseo-yo. geu-rae-seo gim-chi-reul ma-ni meo-geo-yo.]
= Kimchi is delicious. So I eat a lot of Kimchi.

- 많이 = a lot in quantity or frequency

- 먹다 = to eat

5. 저는 한국인이에요. 그래서 김치를 많이 먹어요.
[jeo-neun han-gu-gin-i-e-yo. geu-rae-seo gim-chi-reul ma-ni meo-geo-yo.]
= I'm Korean. So I eat a lot of Kimchi.

- 한국인 = Korean

6. 저는 김치를 많이 먹어요. 그래서 튼튼해요.
[jeo-neun gim-chi-reul ma-ni meo-geo-yo. geu-rae-seo teun-teun-hae-yo.]
= I eat a lot of Kimchi. Therefore I'm strong.

- 튼튼하다 = to be srong

Sample dialogue

Track 06

A: 공부 많이 했어요?
[gong-bu ma-ni hae-sseo-yo?]

B: 아니요. 바빴어요. 그리고 아팠어요.
[a-ni-yo. ba-ppa-sseo-yo. geu-ri-go a-pa-sseo-yo.]

A: 그래서 지금은 괜찮아요?
[geu-rae-seo ji-geu-meun gwaen-cha-na-yo?]

B: 네, 괜찮아요.
[ne, gwaen-cha-na-yo.]

A: Did you study a lot?

B: No. I was busy. And I was sick.

A: So are you okay now?

B: Yes, I'm okay.

Exercises for Level 2 Lesson 3

Please fill in the blanks with "그리고" or "그래서".

1. 책, 연필 (   ) 공책
  = A book, a pencil, and a notebook.

2. 저는 학생이에요. (   ) 돈이 없어요.
  = I am a student. So I don't have money.

3. 김밥은 맛있어요. (   ) 김밥을 자주 먹어요.
  = Kimbap is delicious. So I eat kimbap often.

4. 서울 (   ) 부산
  = Seoul and Busan

5. 아이유는 예뻐요. (   ) 노래도 잘해요.
  = IU is pretty. And she also sings well.

Check the Answers on
p. 177

LESSON 04

〰〰〰

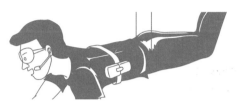

하고, (이)랑

Track 07

In our previous lesson, we introduced the word 그리고. Do you remember what this
[geu-ri-go]
word translates to in English and what it's used for? That's right! It means "and" in
English and is used to link nouns and phrases. However, 그리고 is not the only word
in Korean that means "and" because there are many different ways to say "and" in
Korean. We are introducing two more ways in this lesson, so let's get started!

하고 = and

** 하고 is used like a particle and attached right after a noun without space.
[ha-go]

Ex)

이거 = this, this thing
[i-geo]
이거하고 이거 = this and this
[i-geo-ha-go i-geo]
이거하고 이거 주세요. = Give me this and this.
[I-geo-ha-go I-geo ju-se-yo.]

(이)랑 = and

** If a noun ends in a vowel, you attach 랑 at the end, and if it ends with a final consonant, you use 이랑. This makes it easier to pronounce.
[i-rang]
** (이)랑 and 하고 are almost always interchangeable, but (이)랑 is more colloquial
and casual, so (이)랑 is not very commonly used in formal settings.

Ex)

우유 = milk
[u-yu]

빵 = bread
[ppang]

우유랑 빵 = milk and bread
[u-yu-rang ppang]

빵이랑 우유 = bread and milk
[ppang-i-rang u-yu]

*우유하고 빵 = milk and bread
[u-yu-ha-go ppang]

우유랑 빵 샀어요. = I bought milk and bread.
[u-yu-rang ppang sa-sseo-yo.]

*우유하고 빵 샀어요. = I bought milk and bread.
[u-yu-ha-go ppang sa-sseo-yo.]

빵이랑 우유 샀어요. = I bought bread and milk.
[ppang-i-rang u-yu sa-sseo-yo.]

Another meaning of 하고 *and* (이)랑

Depending on the context of the sentence, both 하고 and (이)랑 can also mean "with", and it is usually very easy to tell whether it is used as "and" or "with".

친구하고 영화 봤어요.
[chin-gu-ha-go yeong-hwa bwa-sseo-yo.]
= I saw a movie with a friend.

** Note that it's unlikely that this sentence means "I watched [a friend and a movie]."

누구랑 갔어요?
[nu-gu-rang ga-sseo-yo?]
= Who did you go with?

If you want to make your meaning clearer, you can add the word 같이 after 하고 or (이)랑. 같이 means "together", so 하고 같이 or (이)랑 같이 means "together with". While "친구하고 영화 봤어요" makes perfect sense, if you say "친구하고 같이 영화 봤어요", it's even better. The same goes for "누구랑 갔어요?" and "누구랑 같이 갔어요?"

Sample Sentences

남자 친구하고 데이트할 거예요.
[nam-ja chin-gu-ha-go de-i-teu-hal geo-ye-yo.]
= I'm going to go on a date with my boyfriend.

선생님하고 밥을 먹을 거예요.
[seon-saeng-nim-ha-go ba-beul meo-geul geo-ye-yo.]
= I'm going to eat with my teacher.

내일 선생님하고 경복궁에 갈 거예요.
[nae-il seon-saeng-nim-ha-go gyeong-bok-gung-e gal geo-ye-yo.]
= I'm going to go to 경복 Palace with my teacher tomorrow.

어제 홍대하고 신촌에 갔어요.
[eo-je hong-dae-ha-go sin-cho-ne ga-sseo-yo.]
= I went to 홍대 and 신촌 yesterday.

** 홍대 and 신촌 are both popular hang out spots for young people.

Sample dialogue

Track 08

A: 어제 영화 봤어요.
[eo-je yeong-hwa bwa-sseo-yo.]

B: 누구랑 봤어요?
[nu-gu-rang bwa-sseo-yo?]

A: 친구랑 봤어요.
[chin-gu-rang bwa-sseo-yo.]

B: 무슨 영화 봤어요?
[mu-seun yeong-hwa bwa-sseo-yo?]

A: 미션 임파서블 봤어요.
[mi-syeon im-pa-seo-beul bwa-sseo-yo.]

A: I saw a movie yesterday.

B: Who did you watch it with?

A: I watched it with my friend.

B: Which movie did you watch?

A: We watched "Mission: Impossible".

Exercises for Level 2 Lesson 4

Fill in the blanks to complete the Korean sentences.

1. 친구(   ) 영화 봤어요.
= I saw a movie with a friend.

2. 누구(   ) 같이 갔어요?
= Who did you go with?

3. 김밥(   ) 라면 좋아해요.
= I like kimbap and ramen noodles.

4. 동생(   ) 스케이트장 갈 거예요.
= I'm going to go ice skating with my younger brother/sister.

5. 노트(   ) 펜 가지고 오세요.
= Please bring your notebook and pen.

Check the Answers on p. 177

LESSON 05

요일

In this lesson, we are going to introduce **the days of the week** in Korean.

월요일 = Monday
[wo-ryo-il]
화요일 = Tuesday
[hwa-yo-il]
수요일 = Wednesday
[su-yo-il]
목요일 = Thursday
[mo-gyo-il]
금요일 = Friday
[geu-myo-il]
토요일 = Saturday
[to-yo-il]
일요일 = Sunday
[i-ryo-il]

The only part that changes in the names for the days of the week is the first letter. The second and the third letters together, means "day of the week" and 월, 화, 수, 목, 금, 토, 일 are the unique names of the days.

Let's glance at the 한자 characters (한자 is the Korean word for Chinese characters) that are used in the names of the days of the week.

月 = 월 = the Moon
   [wol]
火 = 화 = fire
   [hwa]
水 = 수 = water
   [su]
木 = 목 = tree
   [mok]
金 = 금 = gold, metal, iron
   [geum]

土 = 토 = earth, soil, ground
[to]
日 = 일 = the Sun
[il]

Many of the names for the days of the week in Korean are related to the names of the planets in the solar system.

화요일 = Tuesday / 화성 = Mars
[hwa-seong]
수요일 = Wednesday / 수성 = Mercury
[su-seong]
목요일 = Thursday / 목성 = Jupiter
[mok-seon]
금요일 = Friday / 금성 = Venus
[geum-seong]
토요일 = Saturday / 토성 = Saturn
[to-seong]

Sample Sentences

토요일에는 소풍을 갈 거예요.
[to-yo-i-re-neun so-pung-eul gal geo-ye-yo.]
= I'm going to go on a picnic on Saturday.

어제는 신나는 금요일이었어요.
[eo-je-neun sin-na-neun geu-myo-il-i-eo-sseo-yo.]
= Yesterday was a exciting Friday.

저는 월요일에 영화를 봤어요.
[jeo-neun wo-ryo-i-re yeong-hwa-reul bwa-sseo-yo.]
= I watched a movie on Monday.

Sample dialogue

A: 오늘 금요일이에요!
[o-neul geu-myo-i-ri-e-yo!]

B: 네. 정말 좋아요. 주말에 뭐 할 거예요?
[ne. jeong-mal jo-a-yo. ju-ma-re mwo hal geo-ye-yo?]

A: 토요일에는 친구 만날 거예요.
[to-yo-i-re-neun chin-gu man-nal geo-ye-yo.]

B: 일요일에는요?
[i-ryo-i-re-neun-yo?]

A: Today is Friday!

B: Yeah. I'm so happy. What are you going to do on the weekend?

A: On Saturday, I'm going to meet a friend.

B: How about on Sunday?

Track 10

Exercises for Level 2 Lesson 5

Match the Korean words with their English equivalents.

1. 일요일   a. Saturday

2. 화요일   b. Sunday

3. 토요일   c. Thursday

4. 목요일   d. Monday

5. 수요일   e. Friday

6. 월요일   f. Wednesday

7. 금요일   g. Tuesday

Check the
Answers on
p. 177

LESSON 06

~~~~~~~~

그렇지만, 그런데

Track 11

In this lesson, we are introducing two more conjunctive words that you can use at the beginning of sentences. These two words both mean "but" or "however".

그렇지만 = but, however

그런데 = but, however

Ex)

(1)

피곤해요. 그렇지만 영화 보고 싶어요.
[pi-gon-hae-yo. geu-reo-chi-man yeong-hwa bo-go si-peo-yo.]
= I'm tired. But I want to see a movie.

(2)

피곤해요. 그런데 영화 보고 싶어요.
[pi-gon-hae-yo. geu-reon-de yeong-hwa bo-go si-peo-yo.]
= I'm tired. But I want to see a movie.

그렇지만 and **그런데** both mean "but" or "however", but there is some difference
[geu-reo-chi-man]   [geu-reon-de]
between the usages of these two words.

Ex)

(1)

어제 이거 샀어요. 그렇지만 정말 커요.
[eo-je i-geo sa-sseo-yo. geu-reo-chi-man jeong-mal keo-yo.]
= I bought this yesterday. "**그렇지만**" it's really big.

(2)

어제 이거 샀어요. 그런데 정말 커요.
[eo-je i-geo sa-sseo-yo. geu-reon-de jeong-mal keo-yo.]
= I bought this yesterday. "그런데" it's really big.

In sentence (1), **그렇지만** means "but" or "however". The speaker is contrasting the two facts - "having bought this yesterday" and "this being too big" - so it sounds like the speaker is disappointed that it's very big.

In sentence (2), **그런데** means "but", however at the same time, it can also mean "and". If what the speaker is implying is the meaning of "and", the entire sentence can mean "I bought this yesterday, and it's really big." or "I bought this yesterday, and as I found out, it's really big."

In summary,

그렇지만 = "but"
그런데 = "but" or "and", depending on the context

If you want to contrast two sentences and say "A + but + B", you can choose to use either **그렇지만** or **그런데**.

If you want to introduce two actions or states that occurred one after another, and if the first sentence works as background information for the second sentence, only use **그런데**.

어제 학교에 갔어요. 그렇지만 일요일이었어요.
[eo-je hak-gyo-e ga-sseo-yo. geu-reo-chi-man i-ryo-il-i-eo-sseo-yo.]
= I went to school yesterday. But it was Sunday.

어제 학교에 갔어요. 그런데 일요일이었어요.
[eo-je hak-gyo-e ga-sseo-yo. geu-reon-de i-ryo-il-i-eo-sseo-yo.]
= I went to school yesterday. But it was Sunday.

= I went to school yesterday. And by the way, it was Sunday.

= I went to school yesterday. And as I found out after I went, it was Sunday.

As you can see, 그런데 can be used for a wider variety of meanings, and in addition to that, 그렇지만 has a very formal nuance to it. In actual everyday conversations, 그런데 is more commonly used than 그렇지만, and 그렇지만 is more commonly used in written language.

Sample Sentences

1. 어젯밤 늦게 잤어요. 그런데 피곤하지 않아요.
[eo-jet-bam neut-ge ja-sseo-yo. geu-reon-de pi-gon-ha-ji a-na-yo.]
늦게 = late, at a late hour
[neut-ge]
피곤하다 = to be tired
[pi-gon-ha-da]
= I went to bed late last night. But I'm not tired.

2. 저는 매일 운동을 해요. 그런데 살이 빠지지 않아요.
[jeo-neun mae-il un-dong-eul hae-yo. geu-reon-de sa-ri ppa-ji-ji a-na-yo.]
매일 = everyday
[mae-il]
살이 빠지다 = to lose weight
[sa-ri ppa-ji-da]
= I work out everyday. But I don't lose any weight.

3. 저는 친구가 없어요. 그런데 왕따는 아니에요.
[jeo-neun chin-gu-ga eop-seo-yo. geu-reon-de wang-tta-neun a-ni-e-yo.]
왕따 = outcast, loner, someone who is bullied by others
[wang-tta]
= I don't have friends, but I'm not a loner.

Sample dialogue

Track 12

A: 숙제 했어요?
[suk-je hae-sseo-yo?]

B: 네. 그런데 안 가지고 왔어요.
[ne. geu-reon-de an ga-ji-go wa-sseo-yo.]

A: 네? 그래서 집에 다시 갈 거예요?
[ne? geu-rae-seo ji-be da-si gal geo-ye-yo?]

B: 아니요.
[a-ni-yo.]

A: Did you do your homework?

B: Yeah. But I didn't bring it.

A: What? So, are you going to go back home?

B: No.

Exercises for Level 2 Lesson 6

Translate the following words or phrases into Korean:

1. "But" or "however"

(   )

2. "I'm tired. But I'm okay."

(   )

3. "It's good. But it's expensive."

(   )

4. "Yesterday, it rained. But now, it doesn't rain."

(   )

5. "I went to school yesterday. But it was Sunday."

(   )

Check the Answers on p. 177

LESSON 07

한테, 한테서

Track 13   In this lesson, let us learn how to say "to someone" and "from someone". Before you learn these expressions, please remember that when it comes to particles that link words together, there aren't always direct (and correct) translations between English and Korean. It is important to understand the characteristics and roles of these particles and words, rather than just memorizing the similar counterparts in English.

To say "to someone" or "from someone", you can use the words 한테 and 한테서. There are words that have the same characteristics, 에게 and 에게서, but since 에게 and 에게서 are mainly used in written language, let us focus on 한테 and 한테서 in this lesson.

한테 = "to" someone, "from" someone

한테서 = "from" someone

Notice the difference?

Yes, just like you are thinking now, 한테 and 한테서 have mixed meanings and functions, especially 한테, which can mean "to" and "from". The meaning can only be completely understood by examining the context of the sentence.

Although 한테 and 한테서 have the meaning of "to" or "from", you can only use them about people or animals. You can not use these words about objects or places.

- "to a friend" = friend + 한테 (○)
- "to Seoul" = Seoul + 한테 (X)

Sample Sentences

저한테 = to me, from me
[jeo-han-te]
친구한테 = to a friend, from a friend
[chin-gu-han-te]
누구한테 = to whom, from whom
[nu-gu-han-te]

저한테서 = from me
[jeo-han-te-seo]
친구한테서 = from a friend
[chin-gu-han-te-seo]
누구한테서 = from whom
[nu-gu-han-te-seo]

** When used with a verb that already expresses passive voice, 한테 can also mean "by". For example, 맞다 generally means "to be correct", but in another sentence, it can mean "to be beaten" or "to be hit". Therefore, A한테 맞다 can be translated to English as "to be beaten by A".

Sample dialogue

Track 14

A: 왜 동생한테 화냈어요?
[wae dong-saeng-han-te hwa-nae-sseo-yo?]

B: 동생이 저한테 잘못 했어요.
[dong-saeng-i jeo-han-te jal-mot hae-sseo-yo.]

A: 뭘 했는데요?
[mwol haet-neun-de-yo?]

B: 제 옷을 몰래 입었어요.
[je o-seul mol-lae i-beo-sseo-yo.]

A: *Why did you get mad at your brother?*

B: *He did something that upset me.*

A: *What did he do?*

B: *He wore my clothes without telling me.*

Exercises for Level 2 Lesson 7

1. 받다 means "to receive" in English. How do you say "I received it from a friend" in
[bat-da]
Korean?

(   )

2. If 물어보다 is "to ask," how would you say "Whom did you ask?"
[mu-reo-bo-da]

(   )

3. 질문 is "question." How do you write "Do you have a question for me?"
[jil-mun]

(   )

4. Since 남자 친구 is "boyfriend" and 주다 is "to give," how do you say "I will give this
[nam-ja chin-gu]   [ju-da]
to my boyfriend."?

(   )

5. 얻다 is "to obtain; to acquire; to get." How do you write "I got this from my
[eot-da]
friend."?

(   )

*Check the
Answers on
p. 177*

LESSON 08

〰〰〰

한 시, 두 시, 세 시, 네 시, …

Track 15   Now it's TIME to talk about **TIME**!

As we have already introduced through a previous lesson, there are two number systems in Korean. Most of the time, these two number systems are used on separate occasions or they are interchangeable, but when it comes to talking about what time it is, both systems are used at the same time.

Let's review the *native Korean numbers*.

1 하나
   [ha-na]
2 둘
   [dul]
3 셋
   [set]
4 넷
   [net]
5 다섯
   [da-seot]
6 여섯
   [yeo-seot]
7 일곱
   [il-gop]
8 여덟
   [yeo-deol]
9 아홉
   [a-hop]
10 열
    [yeol]
11 열하나
    [yeol-ha-na]
12 열둘
    [yeol-dul]

When you say the hour, you use these native Korean numbers, and numbers 1, 2, 3 and 4 change their forms a little.

Number + 시 = hour

하나 + 시 = 한 시 = 1 o'clock (not 하나 시)
[han si]
둘 + 시 = 두 시 = 2 o'clock (not 둘 시)
[du si]
셋 + 시 = 세 시 = 3 o'clock (not 셋 시)
[se si]
넷 + 시 = 네 시 = 4 o'clock (not 넷 시)
[ne si]
다섯 시 = 5 o'clock
[da-seot si]
여섯 시 = 6 o'clock
[yeo-seot si]
일곱 시 = 7 o'clock
[il-gop si]
여덟 시 = 8 o'clock
[yeo-deol si]
아홉 시 = 9 o'clock
[a-hop si]
열 시 = 10 o'clock
[yeol si]
열한 시 = 11 o'clock
[yeol-han si]
열두 시 = 12 o'clock
[yeol-du si]

Now, let us review some *sino-Korean numbers*.

1 일
[il]
2 이
[i]
3 삼
[sam]
4 사
[sa]
5 오
[o]
6 육
[yuk]
7 칠
[chil]
8 팔
[pal]
9 구
[gu]
10 십
[sip]

Numbers 11 and onward are just combinations of these ten numbers.

When you say the minute, you use these sino-Korean numbers.

Number + 분 = minute
      [bun]

일 분 = 1 minute
[il bun]
이 분 = 2 minutes
[i bun]
오 분 = 5 minutes
[o bun]
십 분 = 10 minutes
[sip bun]
십오 분 = 15 minutes
[si bo bun]
삼십 분 = 30 minutes
[sam-sip bun]
오십오 분 = 55 minutes
[o-si-bo bun]

Let's put the hour and minute together to tell the time.

1:05 = 1 + 시 + 5 + 분 = 한 시 오 분
                              [han si o bun]
1:15 = 1 + 시 + 15 + 분 = 한 시 십오 분
                              [han si si-bo bun]
3:20 = 3 + 시 + 20 + 분 = 세 시 이십 분
                              [se si i-sip bun]
10:00 = 10 + 시 = 열 시
                    [yeol si]
10:30 = 10 + 시 + 30 + 분 = 열 시 삼십 분
                              [yeol si sam-sip bun]

** N o'clock sharp is expressed with the word 정각.
                                            [jeong-gak]
** Instead of 30분 you can say 반, meaning "half".
           [sam-sip-bun]   [ban]

How to ask the time

지금 몇 시예요?
[ji-geum myeot si-ye-yo?]
= What time is it now?

지금 몇 시 몇 분이에요?
[ji-geum myeot si myeot-bun-i-e-yo?]
= What hour and what minute is it?

Sample Sentences

1. **저는 매일 아침 9시까지 출근해요.**
   [jeo-neun mae-il a-chim a-hop-si-kka-ji chul-geun-hae-yo.]
   = I get to work by 9 every morning.

   매일 = everyday
   [mae-il]
   출근하다 = to go to work
   [chul-geun-ha-da]

2. **내일 수업이 4시 반에 끝나요.**
   [nae-il su-eo-bi ne-si ba-ne kkeun-na-yo.]
   = My classes finish at 4:30 tomorrow.

   내일 = tomorrow
   [nae-il]
   수업 = class
   [su-eop]
   끝나다 = to finish
   [kkeut-na-da]

3. **오늘 몇 시에 친구를 만나요?**
   [o-neul myeot si-e chin-gu-reul man-na-yo?]
   = What time do you meet your friend today?

   만나다 = to meet
   [man-na-da]

Sample dialogue

Track 16

A: 지금 몇 시예요?
[ji-geum myeot si-ye-yo?]

B: 지금 여섯 시 사십 분이에요.
[ji-geum yeo-seot si sa-sip bu-ni-e-yo.]

A: 몇 시에 퇴근해요?
[myeot si-e toe-geun-hae-yo?]

B: 일곱시에요. 이십 분 남았어요.
[il-gop-si-e-yo. i-sip bun na-ma-sseo-yo.]

A: What time is it now?

B: It's 6:40 now.

A: What time are you getting off work?

B: At 7. I have 20 minutes left.

Exercises for Level 2 Lesson 8

1. How do you say "What time is it?" in Korean?

(   )

2. How would you say "3 o'clock" in Korean?

(   )

3. In Korean, how do you say "1:15" (time)?

(   )

4. How do you say "5:47" (time)?

(   )

5. How is "10:30" (time) read in Korean?

(   )

Check the
Answers on
p. 178

LESSON 09

개, 명

Track 17 In Korean, there are many words that are used as counting units. In English, you can just say the number and then the word for what you are counting (i.e. a person, two cats, three houses, etc.), but in Korean, you need to use separate counters for different subjects. You can compare the Korean counters to the English words that are used for counting things that are uncountable nouns (i.e. bread, water, butter, etc.)

** Since there are too many counters to remember all at once, it is better to learn them one by one as you practice using certain words.

Ex)
English: number + noun
- a car, two pencils, three books, four people, etc

Korean: noun + number + counter
- "pencil + one + counter for pencil"
- "student + three + counter for people"

There are literally hundreds of counters in the Korean language, but not all of them are always used. As long as the speakers understand each other, some Korean people just use the simplest and easiest counter to count certain words and it does not

confuse anyone. For example, in Korean, a pencil is **연필** and the counter for pencils is
자루. The word **자루** is also used for counting pens, bags containing grain, and knives.
Instead of using the word **자루** all the time for **연필**, many Korean people just use the
general counter for things, which is **개**.
[yeon-pi]
[ja-ru]
[gae]

연필 한 자루 = one pencil
[yeon-pil han ja-ru]
연필 한 개 = one pencil
[yeon-pil han gae]

This does NOT work for all counters. Some common counters are almost never
replaced with **개**. For example, the counter for cars is **대**, and it is never replaced with
개. In other words, changing **연필 한 자루** to **연필 한 개** is okay, but changing **차 한 대**
to **차 한 개** is not okay and considered incorrect.
[dae]
[gae]

This is simply because the counter **대** is more frequently used than the counter **자
루**. However, as a learner of the Korean language, it is good to make a mistake with
counters and be given feedback rather than just choosing not to say anything.

In this lesson, remember these two most frequently used counters, **개** and **명**.

개 in Korean means "a dog", but when it's used as a counter, it is used for counting
things and objects. **명** is used for counting people.
[gae]
[myeong]

When you use counters, most of the time, they are connected to native Korean numbers.

Numbers + **개** (counter for things)
[gae]
1 = **하나** → **한 개**
2 = **둘** → **두 개**
3 = **셋** → **세 개**
4 = **넷** → **네 개**
** Remember this irregularity rule for the numbers 1, 2, 3, 4, and 20?

5 = 다섯 → 다섯 개

6 = 여섯 → 여섯 개

7 = 일곱 → 일곱 개

8 = 여덟 → 여덟 개

9 = 아홉 → 아홉 개

10 = 열 → 열 개

From 11 to 20

열한 개, 열두 개, 열세 개, 열네 개, 열다섯 개, 열여섯 개, 열일곱 개, 열여덟 개, 열아홉 개, 스무 개

From 21 to 30

스물한 개, 스물두 개, 스물세 개, 스물네 개, 스물다섯 개, 스물여섯 개, 스물일곱 개, 스물여덟 개, 스물아홉 개, 서른 개

Ex)

one apple = 사과 + 1 + 개 = 사과 한 개
[sa-gwa]   [gae]   [sa-gwa han gae]

two stones = 돌 + 2 + 개 = 돌 두 개
[dol]   [gae]   [dol du gae]

five balls = 공 + 5 + 개 = 공 다섯 개
[gong]   [gae]   [gong da-seot gae]

how many (things) = 몇 + 개 = 몇 개
[myeot] [gae] [myeot gae]

Now, for people, you use the counter 명.
[myeong]

one person = 한 명
[han myeong]

two students = 학생 + 2 + 명 = 학생 두 명
[hak-saeng]   [myeong] [hak-saeng du myeong]

three friends = 친구 + 3 + 명 = 친구 세 명
[chin-gu]   [myeong] [chin-gu se myeong]

how many (people) = 몇 + 명 = 몇 명
[myeot] [myeong] [myeot myeong]

For people, however, the word for "people" or "person", 사람, is also used when you
[sa-ram]
are generally referring to a relatively small number of people, without specifying who they are.

Ex)

Q: How many people are there?

A: There are 10 people.

= Q: 몇 명 있어요?
[myeot myeong i-sseo-yo?]
= A: 10명 있어요.
[yeol myeong i-sseo-yo.]

= Q: 몇 사람 있어요?
[myeot sa-ram i-sseo-yo?]
= A: 열 사람 있어요. (This is unnatural.)
[yeol sa-ram i-sseo-yo.]
→ A: 두 사람 있어요. (two people - this is okay.)
[du sa-ram i-sseo-yo.]

In case you want to learn more counters in advance, here are a few commonly used ones:

병 = bottles
[byeong]
몇 병 = how many bottles
[myeot byeong]
마리 = animals
[ma-ri]
개 한 마리 = one dog
[gae han ma-ri]
새 한 마리 = one bird
[sae han ma-ri]
오리 세 마리 = three ducks
[o-ri se ma-ri]
대 = cars, punches
[dae]
차 한 대 = one car
[cha han dae]
차 세 대 = three cars
[cha se dae]
권 = books
[gwon]
책 한 권 = one book
[chaek han gwon]
책 두 권 = two books
[chaek du gwon]
장 = paper, pages, tickets
[jang]
종이 한 장 = a sheet of paper
[jong-i han jang]

Sample Sentences

1. **아줌마 김치찌개 한 개 주세요.**
   [a-jum-ma gim-chi-jji-gae han gae ju-se-yo.]
   = Ma'am, give me one kimchi stew.

   찌개 = stew
   [jji-gae]

2. **소주 한 병 주세요.**
   [so-ju han byeong ju-se-yo.]
   = Give me a bottle of soju.

Sample dialogue

Track 18

A: 경은 씨는 가족이 모두 몇 명이에요?
[gyeong-eun ssi-neun ga-jo-gi mo-du myeot myeong-i-e-yo?]

B: 네 명이요. 그리고 강아지도 있어요.
[ne myeong-i-yo. geu-ri-go gang-a-ji-do i-sseo-yo.]

A: 강아지도 있어요?
[gang-a-ji-do i-sseo-yo?]

B: 네. 한 마리 있어요.
[ne. han ma-ri i-sseo-yo.]

A: Kyeong-eun, how many people are there in your family?

B: Four people. And we also have a puppy.

A: You have a puppy, too?

B: Yeah. We have one puppy.

Exercises for Level 2 Lesson 9

Translate the following into Korean.

1. When counting objects: "three things."

(   )

2. When counting people: "five people."

(   )

3. How do you write "three chairs" in Korean? The word for "chair" is 의자.
[ui-ja]

(   )

4. "How many people are there?"

(   )

5. "There are two people."

(   )

Check the
Answers on
p. 178

LESSON 10

-고 있어요

Track 19

Here is another lesson about TENSES! In this lesson, we are introducing how to make sentences in the present progressive form (현재 진행형) in Korean.

Examples of present progressive sentences in English.
1. I'm reading a book.
2. What are you watching?
3. He's helping me a lot.

Basic construction:

- to be -ing = Verb stem + -고 있다
[-go it-da]

보다 = to see
[bo-da]

보고 있다 = to be seeing
[bo-go it-da]

Present progressive:

- am/are/is -ing = Verb stem + -고 있어요
[-go i-sseo-yo]

밖에 비가 오고 있어요. = It is raining outside.
[ba-kke bi-ga o-go i-sseo-yo.]

밖에 눈이 오고 있어요. = It is snowing outside.
[ba-kke nu-ni o-go i-sseo-yo.]

밖에 바람이 불고 있어요. = The wind is blowing outside.
[ba-kke ba-ra-mi bul-go i-sseo-yo.]

Past progressive:

- was/were -ing = Verb stem + -고 있었어요
[-go i-sseo-sseo-yo]

눈이 오고 있었어요. = It was snowing.
[nu-ni o-go i-sseo-sseo-yo.]

비가 오고 있었어요. = It was raining.
[bi-ga o-go i-sseo-sseo-yo.]

58

바람이 불고 있었어요. = The wind was blowing.
[ba-ra-mi bul-go i-sseo-sseo-yo.]

경은 씨가 자고 있었어요. = Kyeong-eun was sleeping.
[kyeong-eun ssi-ga ja-go i-sseo-sseo-yo.]

Future progressive:

- will be -ing = Verb stem + -고 있을 거예요
[-go i-sseul geo-ye-yo]

Past and future progressive sentences are certainly very commonly and are used everyday in Korean, but if you have a very thorough understanding of how to use the present progressive form, past and future progressive forms become very easy to use, too.

When using present progressive tense, there are two important points to remember:

1)
Literal translation between Korean present progressive sentences and English present progressive sentences does not always work, especially if you use the present progressive form in English to indicate the future.

For example, if you say "I'm not going to work tomorrow" in English, you are not talking about the present but the future, so in Korean you can not use the -고 있어요 form.

2)
In everyday conversations, sentences that need to be in the present progressive form do not always take the -고 있어요 form. Korean people often just use the plain present tense form even for sentences that take the present progress tense in English.

Ex)

Instead of saying:

A: **지금 뭐 하고 있어요?** = What are you doing now?
[ji-geum mwo ha-go i-sseo-yo?]
B: **공부하고 있어요.** = I am studying.
[gong-bu-ha-go i-sseo-yo.]

many people say:

A: **지금 뭐 해요?** = What are you doing now?
[ji-geum mwo hae-yo?]
B: **공부해요.** = I am studying.
[gong-bu-hae-yo.]

Sample Sentences

일하다 = to work
[i-ra-da]
일하고 있어요. = I am working.
[i-ra-go i-sseo-yo.]
일하고 있었어요. = I was working.
[i-ra-go i-sseo-sseo-yo.]
일하고 있을 거예요. = I will be working.
[i-ra-go i-sseul geo-ye-yo.]

듣다 = to listen
[deut-da]
듣고 있어요. = I am listening.
[deut-go i-sseo-yo.]
듣고 있었어요. = I was listening.
[deut-go i-sseo-sseo-yo.]
듣고 있을 거예요. = I will be listening.
[deut-go i-sseul geo-ye-yo.]

생각하다 = to think
[saeng-ga-ka-da]
생각하고 있어요. = I am thinking.
[saeng-ga-ka-go i-sseo-yo.]
생각하고 있었어요. = I was thinking.
[saeng-ga-ka-go i-sseo-sseo-yo.]
생각하고 있을 거예요. = I will be thinking.
[saeng-ga-ka-go i-sseul geo-ye-yo.]

졸다 = to doze
[jol-da]
졸고 있어요. = I am dozing.
[jol-go i-sseo-yo.]
졸고 있었어요. = I was dozing.
[jol-go i-sseo-sseo-yo.]
졸고 있을 거예요. = I will be dozing.
[jol-go i-sseul geo-ye-yo.]

Sample dialogue

Track 20

A: 지금 뭐 하고 있어요?
[ji-geum mwo ha-go i-sseo-yo?]

B: 공부 하고 있어요.
[gong-bu ha-go i-sseo-yo.]

A: 무슨 공부 하고 있어요?
[mu-seun gong-bu ha-go i-sseo-yo?]

B: 한국어 공부 하고 있어요.
[han-gu-geo gong-bu ha-go i-sseo-yo.]

A: What are you doing now?

B: I'm studying.

A: What are you studying?

B: I'm studying Korean.

Exercises for Level 2 Lesson 10

Translate the following sentences into Korean:

1. "I am reading a book"?
(읽다 = to read)
[ik-da]

(   )

2. "What are you doing?"

(   )

3. "What were you doing?"

(   )

4. "I was sleeping."

(   )

5. "I will be studying."

(   )

Check the
Answers on
p. 178

Places in Korea
Namsan (남산)

〰〰〰〰

남산 *(Namsan, literally "South Mountain")
stands in the middle of Seoul, surrounded by
major shopping districts and an ever-growing
and modernizing city; however, many genera-
tions ago,* 남산 *marked the southern border
of Seoul.*

*This mountain is easily accessed from many
different points in Seoul because of its central
location. For example, it is a 20-30 minute
walk from Subway lines 1 or 2,* 시청역 *(City
Hall Station) in Jung-gu. It is also right outside
of Subway line 6,* 한강진역 *(Hangangjin Station) and very close to Subway line 3,* 동대입
구역 *(Dongguk University Station)*

There is more to 남산 *than N. Seoul Tower, a.k.a. Namsan
Tower or* 남산타워. *One of the most popular destinations aside of the
tower for tourists and Seoulites alike during the springtime is the Namsan Circular
Road that connects the Namsan Library to the Paljakjung. The cherry blossom trees
that line this road are absolutely beautiful and well worth the hike to get there.*

Almost every part of **남산** is full of lush, natural green landscape that offers a great contrast to the tall buildings and paved streets of the surrounding metropolis. The entire mountain and surrounding area is known as **남산 공원** (Namsan Park). **남산 공원** contains many places of interest, including the National Theater, Namsan Public Library, and several statues in memorial of Korean patriots. The park also contains Paljakjung (an octagonal pavilion), an aquarium, a fountain, and a cable car leading to Seoul Tower.

Since **남산** is, well, a **산**, an added benefit of the placement of this mountain is that you can enjoy hiking without having to travel very far away. While hiking one of the many trails on **남산**, you can enjoy the multitude of trees, plants, and animals as well as take advantage of the exercise equipment You might have to fight off some **아줌마** or **아저씨** to use it, but it'll be a good way to practice your Korean!

남산 is also one of the best places in Seoul to get a panoramic view of the city. Whether you go during the day or at night, you won't be disappointed. There are various photo spots and viewing platforms along the walking trails that give you the best view possible and help you catch spectacular photos of your memories that will last a lifetime.

Written by Stephanie Morris

LESSON 11

자기소개

Now in this lesson, we are going to look at how to do self-introductions in Korean. Through our previous lessons, we have looked at various tenses, sentence patterns, and grammar points. By using what you have already learned, you can already express a lot about yourself. Here in this lesson, we will introduce more vocabulary words and phrases that are specific and absolutely necessary for introducing oneself.

자기소개 *self-introduction*

There are hundreds and thousands of different situations in which one would need to introduce him/herself, but to generalize the self-introduction process by a great deal, you normally deliver these pieces of information:

- name
- age
- place of living
- work
- school
- family members
- hobby
- greetings

You don't have to try to memorize all the expressions necessary for introducing yourself in Korean as the situation might vary and you might have a lot of information and stories unique to yourself, no single detailed chapter on self-introduction can cover everything you need to know.

But basically, the sentences patterns that you get to use a lot are the following:

1. ABC은/는 XYZ이에요. = ABC is XYZ.
[ABC-eun/neun XYZ-i-e-yo.]

Sample Sentences

I'm a student. = 저는 학생이에요.
[jeo-neun hak-saeng-i-e-yo.]
I'm a teacher. = 저는 선생님이에요.
[jeo-neun seon-saeng-ni-mi-e-yo.]
I'm James. = 저는 제임스예요.
[jeo-neun je-im-seu-ye-yo.]
My name is Stephen. = 제 이름은 스티븐이에요.
[je i-reum-eun seu-ti-beu-ni-e-yo.]
My sister's name is Taliana. = 제 여동생 이름은 탈리아나예요.
[je yeo-dong-saeng i-reum-eun tal-li-a-na-ye-yo.]
I am 30 years old. = 저는 30살이에요.
[jeo-neun seo-reun-sa-ri-e-yo.]
My name is Choi Kyeungeun. = 제 이름은 최경은이에요.
[je i-reu-meun choe-gyeong-eu-ni-e-yo.]
My age is a secret. = 제 나이는 비밀이에요.
[je na-i-neun bi-mi-ri-e-yo.]
And I am a Korean teacher. = 그리고 저는 한국어 선생님이에요.
[geu-ri-go jeo-neun han-gu-geo seon-saeng-ni-mi-e-yo.]

2. ABC은/는 XYZ이/가 + VERB = As for ABC, XYZ + VERB.
[ABC-eun/neun XYZ-i/ga]

Sample Sentences

저는 여동생이 있어요. = I have a younger sister. (lit. "As for me, a younger sister exists.")
[jeo-neun yeo-dong-saeng-i i-sseo-yo.]
저는 남동생이 있어요. = I have a younger brother.
[jeo-neun nam-dong-saeng-i i-sseo-yo.]
저는 언니가 있어요. = I have an older sister.
[jeo-neun eon-ni-ga i-sseo-yo.]
저는 취미가 없어요. = I don't have any hobbies. (lit. "As for me, the hobby doesn't exist.")
[jeo-neun chwi-mi-ga eop-sseo-yo.]
저는 취미가 수영이에요. = My hobby is swimming. (lit. "As for me, the hobby, swimming is.")
[jeo-neun chwi-mi-ga su-yeong-i-e-yo.]

3. ABC은/는 XYZ에/에서 + VERB = ABC + VERB + in XYZ.
[ABC-eun/neun XYZ-e/e-seo]

Sample Sentences

저는 서울에 살아요. = I live in Seoul.
[jeo-neun seo-u-re sa-ra-yo.]
저는 은행에서 일해요. = I work in a bank.
[jeo-neun eun-haeng-e-seo il-hae-yo.]
저는 대학교에서 중국어를 가르쳐요. = I teach Chinese in college.
[jeo-neun dae-hak-gyo-e-seo jung-gu-geo-reul ga-reuchyeo-yo.]
저는 미국에서 태어났어요. = I was born in the USA.
[jeo-neun mi-gu-ge-seo tae-eo-na-sseo-yo.]

Some vocabulary words that you might want to know:

나이 = age
[na-i]
취미 = hobby
[chwi-mi]
직장 = workplace
[jik-jang]
직업 = job = 하는 일
[ji-geop]
사는 곳 = place of living
[sa-neun got]
가족 = family
[ga-jok]
친척 = relatives, extended family
[chin-cheok]
대학생 = university student
[dae-hak-saeng]
고등학생 = high school student
[go-deung-hak-saeng]
중학생 = middle school student
[jung-hak-saeng]
초등학생 = elementary school student
[cho-deung-hak-saeng]

Some greetings:

처음 뵙겠습니다. = How do you do?
[cheo-eum boep-ge-sseum-ni-da.]
반갑습니다. = It's nice to meet you.
[ban-gap-seum-ni-da.]
제 명함이에요. = It's my business card.
[je myeong-ham-i-e-yo.]
다음에 또 봬요. = See you again next time.
[da-eu-me tto bwae-yo.]
이야기 많이 들었어요. = I've heard a lot about you.
[i-ya-gi ma-ni deu-reo-sseo-yo.]

Sample dialogue

Track 22

A: 안녕하세요. 저는 동진이 형 동생 석진이에요.
[an-nyeong-ha-se-yo. jeo-neun dong-ji-ni hyeong dong-saeng seok-ji-ni-e-yo.]

B: 반가워요. 이야기 많이 들었어요.
[ban-ga-wo-yo. i-ya-gi ma-ni deu-reo-sseo-yo.]

A: 여기 제 명함이에요.
[yeo-gi je myeong-ha-mi-e-yo.]

B: 아! 고마워요.
[a! go-ma-wo-yo.]

A: Hello. I'm Dongjin's younger brother, Seokjin.

B: Nice to meet you. I've heard a lot about you.

A: This is my business card.

B: Oh, thanks.

Exercises for Level 2 Lesson 11

Translate the following phrases into Korean:

1. "I am a student."

(   )

2. "My name is Minsu."
(**이름** = name, **제 이름** = "My name")
[i-reum]   [je i-reum]

(   )

3. "I am 20 years old."

(   )

4. "I live in Seoul."

(   )

5. "It's nice to meet you."

(   )

Check the
Answers on
p. 178

LESSON 12

날짜

We have already talked about numbers (both sino and native) and we also talked about how to tell time, so why not expand on your knowledge of numbers and talk about dates (**날짜**) this time?

Names of the months

In Korean, the names for the 12 months in a year are very simple. You just have to add the word **월**, which means "month" after every corresponding sino-Korean number.

January 1월
[i rwol]

February 2월
[i-wol]

March 3월
[sa-mwol]

April 4월
[sa-wol]

May 5월
[o-wol]

June 6월
[yu-wol]

July 7월
[chi-rwol]

August 8월
[pa-rwol]

September 9월
[gu-wol]

October 10월
[si-wol]

November 11월
[si-bi-rwol]

December 12월
[si-bi-wol]

Which month: **몇 월**
[myeot wol = myeo-dwol]

Days in a month

The days are also quite easy to say in Korean. All you have to do is say the sino-Korean number and add the word **일**, which means "day" in Korean.
[il]

1일, 2일, 3일, 4일, ..., 29일, 30일, 31일

What date: 며칠
[myeo-chil]

**Note that 몇 월 has 몇 as a standalone word, where as in 며칠, 몇 is combined with 일 to create 며.

What month and what date: 몇 월 며칠
[myeo-dwol myeo-chil]

Sample Sentences

몇 월 며칠이에요?
[myeo-dwol myeo-chil-i-e-yo?]
= "What date is it?"

오늘 몇 월 며칠이에요?
[o-neul myeo-dwol myeo-chil-i-e-yo?]
= What is today's date?

생일이 몇 월 며칠이에요?
[saeng-il-i myeo-dwol myeo-chil-i-e-yo?]
= What date is your birthday?

If you are mentioning a specific day, you can also use the word 언제, which means "when".

생일이 언제예요?
[saeng-il-i eon-je-ye-yo?]
= When is your birthday?

Sample Dialogue

Track 24

A: 생일이 언제예요?
[saeng-i-ri eon-je-ye-yo?]

B: 2월 1일이요.
[i-wol i-ri-ri-yo.]

A: 오늘이 몇 월 며칠이죠?
[o-neu-ri myeot wol myeo-chi-ri-jyo?]

B: 1월 1일이요. 한 달 남았어요.
[i-rwol i-ri-ri-yo. han dal na-ma-sseo-yo.]

A: When is your birthday?
B: It's February first.
A: What's the date today?
B: It's January first. It is one month away.

Exercises for Level 2 Lesson 12

1. In Korean, the word for month is 월. How do you say September?
[wol]

(   )

2. What is the word for "day" or "days" in Korean?

(   )

3. How do you say "September 25th"?

(   )

4. How do you ask "what month?"

(   )

5. How do you ask "what date?"

(   )

6. How do you ask "What date is your birthday?"

(   )

Check the Answers on p. 178

LESSON 13

-도 (Part 1)

Through our previous lesson, we've learned the topic marking particles, -이 and -가, the subject marking particles, -은 and -는, and the object marking particles, -을 and -를. In this lesson, we will be covering one more particle: -도.
[-do]

-도 is used to represent the meaning of **"also" and "too"**.

In English, you generally add the expression "too", "also", or "as well" to the end of the sentence, but sometimes you can add it to the middle. However, in Korean, you always add the particle -도 after the noun.
[-do]

I like it, too.
I think so, too.
I also saw it.

In these sentences, "too" and "also" were used to modify a lot of different things. In the last sentence, the word "also" is modifying "I", and if you translate it literally to Korean, it becomes "저도 봤어요.". You are adding "-도" right after "저" which means "I" in Korean, which modifies "I" just as in the English sentence.

When the particle -도 needs to be attached to a noun or a pronoun that already has a particle behind it, -도 can replace the particle.

Sample Sentences

- I am a student. = 저는 학생이에요.
  [jeo-neun hak-saeng-i-e-yo.]
- I am a student, too. = 저도 학생이에요.
  [jeo-do hak-saeng-i-e-yo.]
  * Note that it's NOT "저는도 학생이에요."

- I brought this. = 이것 가져왔어요.
  [i-geot ga-jyeo-wa-sseo-yo.]
- I brought this, too. = 이것도 가져왔어요.
  [i-geot-do ga-jyeo-wa-sseo-yo.]

- Do you work today? = 오늘 일해요?
  [o-neul i-rae-yo?]
- Do you work today as well? = 오늘도 일해요?
  [o-neul-do i-rae-yo?]

Depending on the location of the particle -도, the meaning of the entire sentence can change.

"Please give me water." is 물 주세요. in Korean.
  [mul ju-se-yo.]
Now let's say you want to say "Give that water to me, as well, not just to other people" then you can say, 저도 물 주세요.
  [jeo-do mul-ju-se-yo.]

"Please give some water to me, too." = 저도 물 주세요.

If you want to say "Give me not only other things, but water as well," then you can say, 저 물도 주세요.
  [jeo mul-do ju-se-yo.]

"Please also give some water to me." = 저 물도 주세요.

In this lesson, we've looked at how to use -도 with nouns and pronouns, but what if you want to say "also" or "too" about verbs? We'll be covering that in our next lesson!

Sample dialogue

Track 26

A: 숟가락 좀 주세요.
[sut-ga-rak jom ju-se-yo.]

B: 여기요.
[yeo-gi-yo.]

A: 젓가락도 좀 주세요.
[jeot-ga-rak-do jom ju-se-yo.]

B: 여기요.
[yeo-gi-yo.]

A: Please give me a spoon.

B: Here you are.

A: Please give me chopsticks as well.

B: Here you are.

Exercises for Level 2 Lesson 13

1. "I am a teacher" is "저는 선생님이에"요.
   [jeo-neun seon-saeng-ni-mi-e-yo.]
   Please write "I am a teacher, too" in Korean.

   (   )

2. "Do you study Korean?" is "한국어 공부해요?"
   [han-gu-geo gong-bu-hae-yo?]
   How do you ask "Do you study Korean, too (in addition to other languages)?"

   (   )

3. "Do you work today?" is "오늘 일해요?"
   [o-neul i-rae-yo?]
   How do you ask "Do you work today as well?"

   (   )

4. "There is water" is "물이 있어요"
   [mu-ri i-sseo-yo.]
   Please write "There is water, too" in Korean.

   (   )

5. Write "give me this, too" in Korean. There can be two ways.

   (   )

Check the Answers on p. 178

LESSON 14

-도 (Part 2)

Track 27 **Using -도 with verbs**

Using -도 with nouns and pronouns is relatively simple since you just have to add -도 after a noun or a pronoun, as explained in the previous lesson.

Let us review.

내일 = Tomorrow
[nae-il]
내일도 = Tomorrow, too.
[nae-il-do]

우유 = Milk
[u-yu]
우유도 = Milk, as well.
[u-yu-do]

나 = Me
[na]
나도 = Me, too.
[na-do]

물 주세요. = Give me water, please.
[mul ju-se-yo.]
물도 주세요. = Give me water, too, please.
[mul-do ju-se-yo.]

내일 갈 거예요. = I will go tomorrow.
[nae-il gal geo-ye-yo.]
내일도 갈 거예요. = I will go (again) tomorrow, too.
[nae-il-do gal geo-ye-yo.]

Now, in order to use -도 with verbs, we need to learn how to change a verb into a noun.

Using - 도 with verbs
= Noun form of the verb + -도 하다

You can't just use -도 with the verb itself, but you can make just a small adjustment by changing the verb into the noun form. By doing this, and adding the verb 하다, you are literally saying "to do + the verb in the noun form + also". It may sound complicated, but this is no different from any other verb conjugation. Just remember -도 하다 as a set.

How do you change a verb into a noun?

There are a few different ways to change a verb into a noun. This is similar to using verbs in the "to do" and "doing" format and also using the nouns for the verbs (i.e. act and action, sing and song, etc.), but today we are looking at just one of those ways.

Adding -기 to the verb stem to change a verb into a noun
Ex)
보다 = to see
[bo-da]
Noun form: 보 + -기 = 보기
[bo-gi]
보다 → 보기도 하다 = to also see, to even see
[bo-gi-do ha-da]

먹다 = to eat
[meok-da]
Noun form: 먹 + -기 = 먹기
[meok-gi]
먹기 → 먹기도 하다 = to also eat, to even eat
[meok-gi-do ha-da]

잡다 = to catch
[jap-da]
 → 잡기도 하다 = to also catch; to even catch
[jap-gi-do ha-da]

팔다 = to sell
[pal-da]
→ 팔기도 하다 = to also sell; to even sell
[pal-gi-do ha-da]

사다 = to buy
[sa-da]
→ 사기도 하다 = to also buy; to even buy
[sa-gi-do ha-da]

** Note: Verbs that are in the form of "Noun + 하다" already (i.e. 공부하다, 청소하다, 노래하다, 준비하다, 요리하다, etc) don't have to be changed in this manner. You can just separate the noun part from 하다 and add -도 after the noun part. (i.e. 공부도 하다, 청소도 하다, 노래도 하다, 준비도 하다, 요리도 하다, etc)

Sample sentences

1. 저는 영어를 가르쳐요.
   [jeo-neun yeong-eo-reul ga-reu-chyeo-yo.]
   = I teach English.

   저는 영어도 가르쳐요.
   [jeo-neun yeong-eo-do ga-reu-chyeo-yo.]
   = I teach English as well.

   저는 영어를 가르치기도 해요.
   [jeo-neun yeong-eo-reul ga-reu-chi-gi-do hae-yo.]
   = I also teach English.

   = I even teach English.

   = I also work as an English teacher.

2. 컴퓨터를 고쳐요.
   [keom-pyu-teo-reul go-chyeo-yo.]
   = I fix computers.

   컴퓨터도 고쳐요.
   [keom-pyu-teo-do go-chyeo-yo.]
   = I fix computers as well.

   컴퓨터를 고치기도 해요.
   [keom-pyu-teo-reul go-chi-gi-do hae-yo.]
   = I also fix computers.

   = I even fix computers.

Sample dialogue

Track 28

A: 비행기에서 주로 뭐 해요?
[bi-haeng-gi-e-seo ju-ro mwo hae-yo?]

B: 영화를 보기도 하고, 잠을 자기도 해요.
[yeong-hwa-reul bo-gi-do ha-go, ja-meul ja-gi-do hae-yo.]

경은 씨는요?
[gyeong-eun ssi-neun-yo?]

A: 저는 계속 자요.
[jeo-neun gye-sok ja-yo.]

B: 기내식도 안 먹어요?
[gi-nae-sik-do an meo-geo-yo?]

A: 아, 밥은 먹어요.
[a, ba-beun meo-geo-yo.]

A: What do you usually do in an airplane?
B: I watch movies or sleep. How about you, Kyeong-eun?
A: I just sleep all the time.
B: You don't even eat in-flight meals?
A: Oh, of course, that I do.

Exercises for Level 2 Lesson 14

1. "To see" is "보다". How do you say "to also see" or "to even see"?
   [bo-da]

(   )

2. "To sell" is "팔다". How do you say "to also sell" or "to even sell"?
   [pal-da]

(   )

3. How do you say "I teach English"?

(   )

4. How do you say "I also teach English" or "I even teach English" with focus being on the act of teaching?

(   )

5. "수학" is "mathematics". How do you say "I also teach math" with focus being on
   [su-hak]
the act of teaching?

(   )

*Check the
Answers on
p. 178*

LESSON 15

-만

Track 29

In this lesson, we are going to learn how to say "**only**" in Korean. There are a few different ways to say "only" in Korean, but the most basic way of saying it is by adding -**만** after a noun, a pronoun, or the noun form (-**기**) of a verb.

1. Adding -**만** after nouns and pronouns
[-man]
이것 + 만 = 이것만 = only this
[i-geot-man]
Ex) 이것만 살 거예요. = I will only buy this.
[i-geot-man sal geo-ye-yo.]

저 + 만 = 저만 = me only, I only
Ex) 저만 들었어요. = Only I heard.
[jeo-man deu-reo-sseo-yo.]

커피 + 만 = 커피만 = only coffee
Ex) 아침에는 커피만 마셔요. = I only drink coffee in the morning.
[a-chi-me-neun keo-pi-man ma-syeo-yo.]
  아침에만 커피(를) 마셔요. = I drink coffee only in the morning.
[a-chi-me-man keo-pi-reul ma-syeo-yo.]

2. Adding -**만** after noun forms of verbs
[-man]
** In order to add -**만** after a verb, you need to change the verb into the noun form using -**기**, and add -**만 하다**. You literally say "I only do + ~ing."

듣다 = to hear; to listen
[deut-da]
듣 + 기 = 듣기 = listening (noun form)
[deut-gi]
듣 + -기 + -만 하다 = 듣기만 하다 = to only listen
[deut-gi-man ha-da]
Ex) 듣기만 했어요. = I only listened (and didn't talk).
[deut-gi-man hae-sseo-yo.]

보다 = to see, to look
[bo-da]
보 + 기 = 보기 = seeing, looking
[bo-gi]

보 + -기 + -만 하다 = 보기만 하다 = to only see, to just look
[bo-ga-man ha-da]

Ex) 보기만 할 거예요. = I will only look (and not touch it).
[bo-gi-man hal geo-ye-yo.]

Sample Sentences

1. **오늘만 일찍 왔어요.**
    [o-neul-man il-jjik wa-sseo-yo.]
    = I got here early only today.

    오늘 = today
    [o-neul]
    일찍 = early
    [il-jjik]
    왔어요. = I came, I got here.
    [wa-sseo-yo.]

2. **맥주만 주문했어요.**
    [maek-ju-man ju-mu-nae-sseo-yo.]
    = I only ordered beer.

    맥주 = beer
    [maek-ju]
    주문했어요. = I ordered.
    [ju-mun-hae-sseo-yo.]

3. **왜 이것만 샀어요?**
    [wae i-geot-man sa-sseo-yo?]
    = Why did you only buy this?

    사다 = to buy
    [sa-da]
    샀어요. = I bought it.
    [sa-sseo-yo.]
    이것 = this, this stuff
    [i-geot]
    왜 = why
    [wae]

4. **어제 놀기만 했어요.**
    [eo-je nol-gi-man hae-sseo-yo.]
    = I did nothing but played.

    놀다 = to play
    [nol-da]
    어제 = yesterday
    [eo-je]

5. **영화는 집에서만 봐요.**
    [yeong-hwa-neun ji-be-seo-man bwa-yo.]
    = I watch movies only at home.

    영화 = a movie
    [yeong-hwa]
    집에서 = at home
    [ji-be-seo]

Sample dialogue

Track 30

A: 공부만 하면 재미 없어요.
[gong-bu-man ha-myeon jae-mi eop-sseo-yo.]

B: 놀기만 하면 안 돼요.
[nol-gi-man ha-myeon an dwae-yo.]

A: 공부도 하고 놀기도 할 거예요.
[gong-bu-do ha-go nol-gi-do hal geo-ye-yo.]

B: 좋아요.
[jo-a-yo.]

A: It's no fun if you only study.

B: You shouldn't only play, either.

A: I'll both study and play.

B: Sounds good.

Exercises for Level 2 Lesson 15

1. What is the word for "only" that you attach after nouns and pronouns?

(   )

2. How do you say "this only"?

(   )

3. "To see" is "보다". How do you say "to only see"?
   [bo-da]

(   )

4. How do you say "I only drink beer"?

(   )

5. "To order" is "주문하다". How do you say "I only ordered beer"?
   [ju-mu-na-da]

(   )

Check the
Answers on
p. 178

LESSON 16

〜〜〜〜〜

조금, 정말, 진짜, 아주, 별로, 전혀

Track 31   In this lesson, let's look at some expressions that can make your sentences richer in context and your emphasis stronger. Sure, you can keep your sentences simple, but when you want to "really" emphasize some points, you might want to know how to say that something is "really" nice, "really" bad, or not good "at all".

Here we will introduce five words - 조금, 아주, 정말, 별로, 전혀 - and how they are used inside sentences.

조금 = a little, a bit, a little bit
[jo-geum]
정말 = really, truly
[jeong-mal]
아주 = very, quite
[a-ju]
별로 = not really, not particularly
[byeol-lo]
전혀 = not at all
[jeon-hyeo]
*조금, 아주, and 정말 can be used with any sentence, but 별로 and 전혀 can only be used with negative sentences.

조금 = a little, a bit, a little bit

Sample Sentences

1. 조금 비싸요.
   [jo-geum bi-ssa-yo.]
= It's a little expensive.

2. 조금만 주세요.
   [jo-geum-man ju-se-yo.]
= Give me only a little bit.

물 조금만 주세요.
[mul jo-geum-man ju-se-yo.]
= Give me only a little bit of water.

소금 조금만 주세요.
[so-geum jo-geum-man ju-se-yo.]
= Give me only a little bit of salt.

** When pronounced quickly, 조금 often becomes 좀 (often pronounced like 쫌) and is frequently written this way, as well.

** Even when you are referring to the meaning of "quite" or "very", you can also use this word, 조금, based on the assumption that the other person understands what you mean. For example, the first sample sentence, "조금 비싸요." can mean either "It's a little bit expensive" or "It's quite expensive."

정말 = really, truly

Sample Sentences

1. 정말 빨라요.
[jeong-mal ppal-la-yo.]
= It's really fast.

2. 정말 이상해요.
[jeong-mal i-sang-hae-yo.]
= It's really strange.

** A word that has almost the same meaning as 정말 is 진짜. It is considered a little
[jin-jja]
less formal than 정말.

** Whereas the other words introduced here are used to describe the extent to which something is done or to describe the intensity of a certain state (i.e. very 'good', a little 'expensive' or quite 'fast'), 정말 and 진짜 can also be used to just express whether or not what's being said is true or not. (i.e. I 'really' did it.)

Sample Conversation

A: 제가 방 청소했어요! = I cleaned up my room!
[je-ga bang cheong-so-hae-sseo-yo!]
B. 아... 진짜? = Oh, really?
[ah... jin-jja?]
A: 예, 진짜! 보고 싶어요? = Yeah, really! Do you want to see it?
[ye, jin-jja! Bo-go si-peo-yo?]

아주 = very, quite

Sample Sentences

1. 아주 맛있어요.
[a-ju ma-si-sseo-yo.]
= It's very delicious.

2. 아주 멀어요.
[a-ju meo-reo-yo.]
= It's very far away.

** 아주 is the most standard way of saying "very" in the written form, but more often than not, in spoken Korean, 아주 is often replaced with 정말 or 진짜.
[jeong-mal] [jin-jja]

별로 = not really; not particularly

** 별로 is always used in negative sentences, regardless of whether the verb that comes after it has a negative or a positive meaning.
** Unlike the words such as "not really" and "not particularly", in Korean, you also have to include 안, in other parts of the sentence to actually make a sentence negative instead of just using 별로. So if you say "내일은 별로..", the other person that you are talking to will be able to guess that your sentence ending will be something of a negative meaning.

Sample Sentences

1. 별로 안 비싸요.
[byeol-lo an bi-ssa-yo.]
= It's not so expensive.

2. 별로 재미없어요.
[byeol-lo jae-mi-eop-seo-yo.]
= It's not that interesting.

** Note that 재미없어요 is one word, but it has the part '없어요' inside the word, so it's possible to say 별로 재미없어요.

3. 별로 안 나빠요.
[byeol-lo an na-ppa-yo.]
= It's not too bad. (It's not the worst, but it's still bad. Note: this does not mean the same thing as the English phrase "it's not bad".)

** Even if the word 나쁘다 has a negative meaning, the construction '별로 나쁘다' does not work.

전혀 = not at all

Sample Sentences

1. **전혀 안 바빠요.**
[jeon-hyeo an ba-ppa-yo.]
= I'm not busy at all.

2. **전혀 안 더워요.**
[jeon-hyeo an deo-wo-yo.]
= It's not hot at all.

** In spoken Korean, the expression **하나도** is use more commonly than **전혀**.
[ha-na-do]

Sample dialogue

Track 32

A: 정말 배고파요.
[jeong-mal bae-go-pa-yo.]

B: 점심 안 먹었어요?
[jeom-sim an meo-geo-sseo-yo?]

A: 먹었어요. 조금.
[meo-geo-sseo-yo. jo-geum.]

B: 저는 진짜 많이 먹어서 지금 배 별로 안 고파요.
[jeo-neun jin-jja ma-ni meo-geo-seo ji-geum bae byeol-lo an go-pa-yo.]

A: I'm so hungry.

B: Haven't you had lunch?

A: I have. A little.

B: I ate too much, so I'm not that hungry now.

Exercises for Level 2 Lesson 16

1. "It's a bit expensive."

(   )

2. "It's very interesting."

(   )

3. "It's really strange."

(   )

4. "It's not that expensive."

(   )

5. "It's not interesting at all."

(   )

Check the
Answers on
p. 178

LESSON 17
〰〰〰

-ㄹ 수 있다/없다

Track 33 After studying with the previous lessons, you can now form various sentence structures in Korean. Now it's time to look at how to say that you "can" or "cannot" do something.

The sentence structure you can use to say that you "can" do something is:
-(으)ㄹ 수 있다

Ex)
보다 = to see
→ 보 + -ㄹ 수 있다 = 볼 수 있다 = can see
[bol su it-da]

먹다 = to eat
→ 먹 + -을 수 있다 = 먹을 수 있다 = can eat
[meo-geul su it-da]

** Verb stems ending in a vowel are followed by -ㄹ 수 있다 and verb stems ending with a consonant are followed by -을 수 있다. The difference is whether you have the extra 으 or not in front of -ㄹ 수 있다, for the ease of pronunciation.

In -(으)ㄹ 수 있다, the word 수 literally means an 'idea' or a 'way' for solving a problem or for getting something done. This is the same meaning as 방법(= a method), so
[-(eu)l su it-da]   [su]
-(으)ㄹ 수 있다 literally means "to have a way or an idea for doing" something.

Therefore, when you do NOT have "a way or an idea" for doing something, it means you can NOT do it, and in Korean it becomes -(으)ㄹ 수 없다, using 없다, the opposite word of 있다.

Ex)

자다 = to sleep

→ 자 + -ㄹ 수 없다 = 잘 수 없다 = cannot sleep
[jal su eop-da]

⟵⟶ 잘 수 있다 = can sleep
[jal su it-da]

잡다 = to catch

→ 잡 + -을 수 없다 = 잡을 수 없다 = cannot catch
[ja-beul su eop-da]

⟵⟶ 잡을 수 있다 = can catch
[ja-beul su it-da]

Another way to say -(으)ㄹ 수 없다 is by using the word 못 before a verb.

-(으)ㄹ 수 없다 is the most basic way to express "cannot", but it is not always used in spoken Korean. A more common way to say "cannot" or "to be unable to" in spoken Korean is by adding 못 before a verb.

갈 수 없다 = 못 가다 [verb: 가다] = cannot go
볼 수 없다 = 못 보다 [verb: 보다] = cannot see
먹을 수 없다 = 못 먹다 [verb: 먹다] = cannot eat
할 수 없다 = 못 하다 [verb: 하다] = cannot do

Sample Sentences

운전 할 수 있어요?
[un-jeon hal su i-sseo-yo?]
= Can you drive? (lit. "Can you do driving?")

일본어 할 수 있어요?
[il-bo-neo hal su i-sseo-yo?]
= Can you speak Japanese? (lit. "Can you do Japanese?")

이거 읽을 수 있어요?
[i-geo il-geul su i-sseo-yo?]
= Can you read this?

못 읽어요.
[mot il-geo-yo.]
= I can't read it.

지금 못 만나요.
[ji-geum mot man-na-yo.]
= I can't meet you now.

Sample dialogue

Track 34

A: 수영할 수 있어요?
[su-yeong-hal su i-sseo-yo?]

B: 아니요. 경은 씨는요?
[a-ni-yo. gyeong-eun ssi-neun-yo?]

A: 저도 못 해요.
[jeo-do mot hae-yo.]

B: 같이 배울래요?
[ga-chi bae-ul-lae-yo?]

A: Can you swim?

B: No, I can't. How about you, Kyeong-eun?

A: I can't, either.

B: Do you want to learn with me?

Exercises for Level 2 Lesson 17

1. "To go" is "**가다**". How do you say "I can go."?
   [ga-da]

(   )

2. How do you say "I can't do it."?

(   )

3. How do you say "Can you do this?"

(   )

4. How do you say "Can we meet now?"

(   )

5. "To swim" is "**수영하다**". How do you say "Can you swim?"
   [su-yeong-ha-da]

(   )

Check the
Answers on
p. 179

LESSON 18

〰〰〰

잘하다, 못하다

Track 35 In the previous lesson, we learned how to say that you "can" or "cannot" do something. Let's expand your Korean skills by taking a look at how to say that you are "good" or "bad" at doing something.

The basic construction for saying "to do something" is [object] + -을/를 (= object marker) + 하다 (= to do), and to this, you add 잘 or 못.

[jal] [mot]

~을/를 잘하다 = **to be good at ~** (lit. to do ~ well)

~을/를 못하다 = **to be poor at ~** (lit. to do ~ poorly)

Ex)

노래 = singing; song

[no-rae]
노래를 잘하다 = to be good at singing; to sing well

[no-rae-reul ja-ra-da]

요리 = cooking, dish

[yo-ri]
요리를 못하다 = to be poor at cooking; to cook poorly

[yo-ri-reul mo-ta-da]

Since 못하다 can also mean "to be unable to do" or "cannot do" something, 잘 is often added in front of this to make the meaning clearer. By saying "**잘 못하다**", you

[jal]
literally say that you "cannot do something well" or "are unable to do something well", which is similar to being poor at it.

요리를 못하다 = "to be poor at cooking" OR "cannot cook"

요리를 잘 못하다 = "to be poor at cooking"

Ex)

수영 = swimming
[su-yeong]

수영을 잘하다
[su-yeong-eul ja-ra-da]
= to be good at swimming

수영을 못하다
[su-yeong-eul mo-ta-da]
= to be bad at swimming

OR

= cannot swim

수영을 잘 못하다
[su-yeong-eul jal mo-ta-da]
= to be bad at swimming

*You have to be careful when you say "잘 못하다". If you say "잘 못하다" with a space between 잘 and 못하다, that's "to be poor at something", but if you say "잘못 하다", it means "to do something in the wrong way" or even "to make a mistake". So be careful with the accent! ;-)

Are 잘 and 못 (or 잘 못) only used with -하다 verbs?

No. Other types of verbs can be used with 잘 and 못 as well. Since the first parts of most -하다 verbs are nouns, it is easy to detach the noun part from -하다 and add 잘, 못, or 잘 못 in front of -하다, but for other types of verbs that are not in the "noun + -하다" form, you just add 잘, 못, or 잘 못 in front of the verb with a space in between.

잘 달리다 = to run well, to be good at running

잘 쓰다 = to write well, to be good at writing

However, when a verb is used only on its own like this, very often, the meaning isn't very clear (i.e. 쓰다 can be both 'to write' and 'to use') and the phrase sounds incomplete, so a noun is added to the phrase to pair up with the verb.

잘 쓰다 → 글을 잘 쓰다 (= You are a good writer. You are very good at writing stuff.)
[lit. "to write well"]
글 is a noun for "a piece of writing" or "a composition", it's basically written text.

잘 쓰다 → 글씨를 잘 쓰다 (= You are good at handwriting.)
[lit. "to write writing/letters well"]
Here, the word 글씨, meaning "writing" or "letters", was used to make the meaning of "writing"
more clear, and prevent people from thinking that it might mean "to use".

잘 달리다 → 달리기를 잘하다 (= You are good at running.)
[lit. "to do running well"]
Here, 달리다 was changed to its noun form, 달리기, and was followed by 잘하다.

Sample Sentences

저는 노래를 잘 못해요.
[jeo-neun no-rae-reul jal mo-tae-yo.]
= I can't sing well. / I'm not good at singing.

제 친구는 수영을 잘해요.
[je chin-gu-neun su-yeong-eul ja-rae-yo.]
= My friend is good at swimming.

저는 퍼즐을 잘 풀어요.
[jeo-neun peo-jeu-reul jal pu-reo-yo.]
= I am good at solving puzzles.

저는 글씨를 잘 못 써요.
[jeo-neun geul-ssi-reul jal mot sseo-yo.]
= My handwriting is not good.

저는 글을 잘 못 써요.
[jeo-neun geu-reul jal mot sseo-yo.]
= I'm not good at writing.

매운 거 잘 먹어요?
[mae-un geo jal meo-geo-yo?]
= Are you good at eating spicy food?

Sample dialogue

Track 36

A: 경은 씨, 수영 잘해요?
[gyeong-eun ssi, su-yeong ja-rae-yo?]

B: 아니요. 잘 못해요. 석진 씨는요?
[a-ni-yo. jal mo-tae-yo. seok-jin ssi-neun-yo?]

A: 저는 수영 잘해요.
[jeo-neun su-yeong ja-rae-yo.]

B: 우와! 부러워요.
[u-wa! bu-reo-wo-yo.]

A: Kyeong-eun, are you good at swimming?

B: No, I'm not that good at it. How about you, Seokjin?

A: I'm good at swimming.

B: Wow! I'm jealous.

Exercises for Level 2 Lesson 18

1. "To do" is "하다" [ha-da]. How do you say "to do something well" or "to be good at doing something"?

(   )

2. And how do you say "to be bad at doing something"?

(   )

3. What can you say to imply that you're either bad at doing something or unable to do something?

(   )

4. Write "I am good at swimming" in Korean.

(   )

5. How do you say "I'm not good at singing"?

(   )

Check the Answers on p. 179

LESSON 19
〜〜〜〜〜

-는 것

In Level 2 Lesson 14, we learned how to add the meaning of "also" to a verb in Korean. Let's review a little: In order to add -도 to a verb, you must change the verb into the noun form by adding -기 to the verb stem, add the -도, and end with 하다 (i.e. 먹기도 해요.)

In this lesson, we are going to look at **a more general way of making nouns out of action verbs**. Understanding how this works will help you a great deal in understanding how to form other various expressions in Korean.

-는 것

This is the most basic and general way of changing an action verb into a noun. 것 originally means "a thing", "an object", or "stuff", but when it is used like this, it can also mean "a fact" or "an act".

Construction:
- **Verb stem + -는 것**
 [-neun geot]

By changing verbs into nouns, [verb stem + -는 것] can take many different meanings:
1. "doing" something
2. the act of "doing" something
3. the thing that you "do"
4. what you "do"
5. the fact that you do something

104

Ex)

보다 = to see
[bo-da]
보는 것 = seeing; the act of seeing; the thing that you see; what I watch
[bo-neun geot]
가다 = to go
[ga-da]
가는 것 = going; the act of going
[ga-neun geot]
먹다 = to eat
[meok-da]
먹는 것 = eating; the act of eating; the thing that you eat; what you eat
[meok-neun geot]
사다 = to buy
[sa-da]
사는 것 = buying; the act of buying; the thing that you buy; what you buy
[sa-neun geot]

Note that this is only for verbs in the present tense. We will look at how to say things like "the thing you will buy" or "the thing you bought" in our future lessons, but for your reference, you use -(으)ㄴ 것 for the past tense and -(으)ㄹ 것 for the future tense.

산 것 = what you bought
사는 것 = what you buy
살 것 = what you will buy

먹은 것 = what you ate
먹는 것 = what you eat
먹을 것 = what you will eat

-는 것 *vs* -는 거

-는 것 is the standard form, but often times the form -는 거 is used because it is easier to pronounce. It is not, however, ever used in very formal situations.

지금 듣는 것은 노래예요.
[ji-geum deut-neun geo-seun no-rae-ye-yo.]
= What I am listening to now is a song.
→ 지금 듣는 거는 노래예요.

오늘 만나는 것 알아요?
[o-neul man-na-neun geot a-ra-yo?]
= Do you know that we are meeting today?

→ 오늘 만나는 거 알아요?

매운 것 잘 먹어요?
[mae-un geot jal meo-geo-yo?]
= Are you good at eating spicy foods?

→ 매운 거 잘 먹어요?

Sample Sentences

1. 제 취미는 영화 보는 거예요.
   [je chwi-mi-neun yeong-hwa bo-neun geo-ye-yo.]
= My hobby is watching movies.

2. 요즘 공부하는 거는 뭐예요?
   [yo-jeum gong-bu-ha-neun geo-neun mwo-ye-yo?]
= Recently, what is it that you are studying?

= 요즘 뭐 공부해요?

3. 저는 친구랑 수다떠는 거를 좋아해요.
   [jeo-neun chin-gu-rang su-da-tteo-neun geo-reul jo-a-hae-yo.]
= I like chitchatting with my friends.

Sample dialogue

Track 38

A: 한국어 공부하는 거 힘들어요?
[han-gu-geo gong-bu-ha-neun geo him-deu-reo-yo?]

B: 아니요. 재밌어요.
[a-ni-yo. jae-mi-sseo-yo.]

A: 아, 정말요?
[a, jeong-mal-yo?]

B: 네. 그런데 쓰는 것은 정말 어려워요.
[ne. geu-reon-de sseu-neun geo-seun jeong-mal eo-ryeo-wo-yo.]

A: Is studying Korean tough?

B: No, it's fun.

A: Oh, really?

B: Yes, but writing it is really difficult.

Exercises for Level 2 Lesson 19

1. "To eat" is "먹다". How do you say "eating," "the act of eating," or "what
   [meok-da]
you eat" in Korean?

(   )

2. "To go" is "가다". How do you say "going" or "the act of going" in Korean?
   [ga-da]

(   )

3. How do you say "I like reading books"?

(   )

4. How do you say "I don't like spicy things"?

(   )

5. How do you say "My hobby is watching movies"?

(   )

Check the
Answers on
p. 179

LESSON 20

~~~~~~~~

-아/어/여야 되다/하다

Track 39

In this lesson, we are going to take a look at how to say that you "**have to**" or "**should**" do something in Korean. The construction itself is quite simple to understand: you take the verb stem of a verb and a verb ending that makes the sentences take the meaning of "have to" or "should".

to have to, should, must
= **verb stem +** -아/어/여 + -야 되다/하다

Ex)
자다 = to sleep
[ja-da]
자 + -아/어/여 + -야 되다/하다
→ 자 + "-아" + -야 되다/하다 (You choose "-아" because 자 ends with the vowel " ㅏ ")
→ 자야 되다/하다 (You then drop the -아 because it's the same same as " ㅏ ")
→ 자야 되다 and 자야 하다 are the same thing.

쓰다 = to use; to write
[sseu-da]
쓰 + -아/어/여 + -야 되다/하다
→ 쓰 + "-어" + -야 되다/하다 (You choose "-어" because 쓰 doesn't end in " ㅏ " or "ㅗ")
→ 써야 되다/하다 (쓰 + 어 together change to '써')
→ 써야 되다 and 써야 하다 mean the same thing.

The construction is basically one of the following:
1. verb stems ending in vowels 'ㅏ' or 'ㅗ' + -아야 되다/하다

2. verb stems ending in other vowels + -어야 되다/하다

3. 하 + -여야 되다/하다

However, it is more important to understand WHY -아/어/여야 되다/하다 means "to have to" or "should".

In order to understand this, we can look at the structure in two separate parts.

1. -아/어/여 + -야
This part means "only when _____ is done" or "only when you do _____".

2. 되다 or 하다
되다 means "to be done" or "to be possible" and 하다 means "to do" something.

Therefore, if you put 1 and 2 together, it takes the meaning of "only when you do _____, it works", "only when you do this, everything is alright", or "only if _____ is done, it's okay." Thus, -아/어/여야 되다/하다 takes the meaning of "to have to" or "should."

Q: What is the difference between 하다 and 되다 here?
A: The only difference is that using 되다 is more common in colloquial situations.

Sample sentences

1. 집에 가야 돼요.
   [ji-be ga-ya dwae-yo.]
   = I have to go home.

2. 저는 뭐 해야 돼요?

[jeo-neun mwo hae-ya dwae-yo?]

= What should I do?

3. 언제까지 여기에 있어야 돼요?

[eon-je-kka-ji yeo-gi-e i-sseo-ya dwae-yo?]

= Until when should I be here?

4. 누구한테 줘야 돼요?

[nu-gu-han-te jwo-ya dwae-yo?]

= Who should I give this to?

5. 어디에서 사야 돼요?

[eo-di-e-seo sa-ya dwae-yo?]

= Where should I buy it?

Sample dialogue

Track 40

A: 저 집에 가서 숙제 해야 돼요.
[jeo ji-be ga-seo suk-je hae-ya dwae-yo.]

B: 언제까지 해야 돼요?
[eon-je-kka-ji hae-ya dwae-yo?]

A: 내일까지 해야 돼요.
[nae-il-kka-ji hae-ya dwae-yo.]

A: I have to go home and do my homework.

B: When do you have to finish it by?

A: I have to finish it by tomorrow.

Exercises for Level 2 Lesson 20

1. What is the difference between 하다 and 되다?

(   )

Translate the following to Korean:

2. "I have to go."

(   )

3. "I have to write" or "I have to use."

(   )

4. "I have to do it now."

(   )

5. "Where do you have to go tomorrow?"

(   )

Check the
Answers on
p. 179

Korean Food Recipes
Kimchi Fried Rice

~~~~~~~~~~

김치 볶음밥 *is super delicious, super easy to make, and it fries up so quickly that you'll barely have time to say "*한국 음식 진짜 좋아해요!*" (I really like Korean food!) before it's cooked!*

One of the best things about Korean cooking is that you can add your own flair to it. If you want to add corn, do it! Want to add SPAM or 두부 *(tofu) ? Go ahead!*

This is a pretty basic recipe for 김치 볶음밥 *and makes 2 very generous servings.*

Let's get cooking!

You will need :

후라이팬 *(fry pan)*
2 cups (or 2 rice bowls) of cooked 밥 *(rice)*
1 cup of 김치 *(kimchi)—do not drain or squeeze the liquid!*
½ of a 양파 *(onion)*
1 clove of 마늘 *(garlic)*
1-2 Teaspoon of 고추장 *(gochujang – a.k.a. hot pepper paste) (1 Tablespoon if you like it medium-hot, and 2 Tablespoons if you'd like a death sentence.)*
1 Tablespoon of 간장 *(soy sauce)*
2 teaspoons of 설탕 *(sugar)*
2 tablespoons of 김치 *juice from the jar*
2 달걀 *(egg)*
1 Teaspoon 참기름 *(sesame oil)*
2 Tbsp oil for frying *(vegetable, canola, olive..etc.)*
깨소금 *(sesame seeds) for garnish*
1 파 *(green onion) for garnish*

Directions

1. Chop 파, mince 1 clove of 마늘, rough chop 1 cup of 김치, Cut 양파. Set aside.
2. Heat 1Tbsp of oil in the 후라이팬 over medium heat.
3. Once the oil is heated, fry the 2 달걀. Traditionally, the 달걀 is served sunny-side up. ****
(****Note: You can cook the 달걀 before you start to cook the rice, or you can cook it after you've plated the rice and wiped the 후라이팬 clean, or you can cook the 달걀 in a separate 후라이팬. Basically, you can cook the 달걀 whenever you want and however you want!)
4. Heat the remaining 1 Tbsp of oil in the 후라이팬.
5. When the oil is heated, add 마늘 and 양파. Saute until you can smell them (about 1 minute).
6. Add chopped 김치. Fry for 2-3 minutes.
7. Add 밥 and stir well to combine.
8. Turn down the heat (medium-low) and add 김치 juice, 간장, 설탕, and 고추장.
9. Stir/fold to make sure it mixes well with the rice.
10. Turn off the heat and add 1 teaspoon of 참기름. Mix well.
11. Put the 김치 볶음밥 on a plate or in a bowl and put a fried egg on top. Garnish with 깨소금 and chopped 파!

Voila! Delicious 김치 볶음밥!

Written by Stephanie Morris

***

You're half way finished with Level 2!
Cook up some 김치 볶음밥 to replenish your strength and power
through the rest of this book!

LESSON 21

〰〰〰

~보다 더

Track 41 After studying with this lesson, you can compare two things or people in Korean by saying that something is better than something else, or someone is taller than someone else.

How to say "more" in Korean

In Korean, the word for "more" is 더. In English, relatively short words change their
[deo]
forms instead of having the word "more" in front of them, such as "shorter", "hotter", "faster". In Korean, however, all words just have 더 in front of them.

Ex)
빠르다 = to be fast
[ppa-reu-da]
더 빠르다 = to be faster
[deo ppa-reu-da]

비싸다 = to be expensive
[bi-ssa-da]
더 비싸다 = to be more expensive
[deo bi-ssa-da]

예뻐요. = It's pretty. / You're pretty. / She's pretty.
[ye-ppeo-yo.]
더 예뻐요. = It's prettier. / You're prettier. / She's prettier.
[deo ye-ppeo-yo.]

How to say "than" in Korean

The word for "than" or "compared to" is 보다. The basic construction for this is not
[bo-da]
very complicated, but the word order in Korean is completely different from English.
Let us compare the two.

English: A watermelon is bigger than an apple.
Korean: 수박은 사과보다 더 커요.
[su-ba-geun sa-gwa-bo-da deo keo-yo.]

** In the English sentence above, the word "than" comes BEFORE "apple", but in Korean, the
word -보다 (which means "than") comes AFTER 사과, which means "apple".
[bo-da]   [sa-gwa]

Construction:
than A = A보다
more (verb/adjective/adverb) **than A** = A보다 더 (verb/adjective/adverb)

Ex)
1) to be big = 크다
        [keu-da]
    to be bigger = 더 크다
        [deo keu-da]
    It's bigger. = 더 커요.
        [deo keo-yo.]
    It's bigger than this one. = 이거보다 더 커요.
        [i-geo-bo-da deo keo-yo.]

2) to be nice = 좋다
        [jo-ta]
    to be nicer = 더 좋다
        [deo jo-ta]
    It's nicer. = 더 좋아요.
        [deo jo-a-yo.]
    It's nicer than this one. = 이거보다 더 좋아요.
        [i-geo-bo-da deo jo-a-yo.]

    to be nice (to people) = 착하다
        [cha-ka-da]
    to be nicer = 더 착하다
        [deo cha-ka-da]
    현우 is nicer. = 현우 씨는 더 착해요.
        [hyeo-nu ssi-neun deo cha-kae-yo.]
    현우 is nicer than 경은. = 현우 씨는 경은 씨보다 더 착해요.
        [hyeo-nu ssi-neun gyeong-eun ssi-bo-da deo cha-kae-yo.]

** 더 is not always necessary in Korean sentences. In English, it would be weird if you said
[deo]
"She's busy than me" instead of "She's busier than me," but in Korean, the meaning is perfectly

clear even without the word 더.
[deo]

Sample Sentences

1. 오늘은 어제보다 더워요.
[o-neu-reun eo-je-bo-da deo-wo-yo.]
= Today is hotter than yesterday.

2. 영어는 한국어보다 어려워요.
[yeong-eo-neun han-gu-geo-bo-da eo-ryeo-wo-yo.]
= English is more difficult than Korean.

3. 어제보다 일찍 갈 거예요.
[eo-je-bo-da il-jjik gal geo-ye-yo.]
= I'm going to go earlier than yesterday.

4. 현정 씨가 저보다 더 잘 해요.
[hyeon-jeong ssi-ga jeo-bo-da deo jal hae-yo.]
= Hyeonjeong is better than me (at doing that).

5. 저는 책을 읽는 것보다 사는 것을 더 좋아해요.
[jeo-neun chae-geul il-neun geot-bo-da saneun geo-seul deo jo-a-hae-yo.]
= I like buying books more than reading books.

Sample dialogue

Track 42

A: 오늘이 어제보다 더 추워요.
[o-neu-ri eo-je-bo-da deo chu-wo-yo.]

B: 그런데 내일은 더 추울 거예요.
[geu-reon-de nae-i-reun deo chu-ul geo-ye-yo.]

A: 진짜요? 너무 싫어요.
[jin-jja-yo? neo-mu si-reo-yo.]

A: Today, it is colder than yesterday.

B: But tomorrow, it is going to be even colder.

A: Really? I hate it.

Exercises for Level 2 Lesson 21

1. "To be fast" is "빠르다". How do you say "to be faster"?
   [ppa-reu-da]

(   )

2. "To be good" is "좋다". How do you say "to be better"?
   [jo-ta]

(   )

3. How do you say "Coffee is more expensive than water"?

(   )

4. How do you say "This book is more interesting than that book"?

(   )

5. How do you say "I came here earlier than yesterday"?

(   )

Check the Answers on p. 179

LESSON 22

좋다 vs 좋아하다

Track 43   One of the expressions that you have probably encountered on your Korean language learning journey is the verb 좋다, which generally means "to be good". However, you might have come across a few instances where 좋다 takes on the meaning of "to like".
[jo-ta]

Ex)
한국어 좋아요.
[han-gu-geo jo-a-yo.]
= I like the Korean language.

이거 좋아요.
[i-geo jo-a-yo.]
= I like this.

동방신기 좋아요.
[dong-bang-sin-gi jo-a-yo.]
= I like DBSK.

Even though the verb 좋다 in the examples above is used to mean "to like", the verb originally means "to be good". In principle, the nouns (**한국어, 이거, 동방신기**) are subjects of the sentences.

Therefore, the particles that are hidden after the nouns are NOT object marking particles, but in fact, they are subject marking particles.

한국어 좋아요.
→ 한국어를 좋아요. (x)
→ 한국어가 좋아요. (o)

In this sentence, you are literally saying that "Korean is good, likable, enjoyable, and preferable FOR YOU.

The difference between 좋다 and 좋아하다

If you want to express more precisely that you like something, you can use the verb 좋아하다, which can be translated as "to like", "to be fond of", or "to enjoy doing something". The meanings might be similar, but since 좋다 means "to be good", the noun that goes with it is the subject of the sentence, and for 좋아하다, the noun that goes with it is the object.

한국어 좋아해요.
→ 한국어를 좋아해요. (o)
→ 한국어가 좋아해요. (x)

If you just drop the particles altogether, you don't have to worry about this difference.

1) 동방신기 좋아요.
2) 동방신기 좋아해요.

Sentence number 1) and 2) have the same meaning, but if you want to specify what is good and who likes whom, you might want to add the particles.

3) 동방신기가 좋아요.
4) 동방신기를 좋아요.

Sentence number 3) means that you like DBSK Sentence number 4) is not correct because 좋다 is not a verb that can have an object.

5) 동방신기를 좋아해요.
6) 동방신기가 좋아해요.

Sentence number 5) means that you (or someone else) like DBSK, and (IMPORTANT!) sentence number 6) means that DBSK likes something or someone. The subject of the sentence is DBSK, so you need to add what it is that DBSK likes.

Descriptive verbs + ~하다 combination

Construction:
Verb stem + -아/어/여 + -하다

As in the case of 좋다 and 좋아하다, there can be many pairs of words that seem similar at first but are actually different in usage.

Ex)
1) 싫다 / 싫어요.
[sil-ta]   [si-reo-yo.]
= to be unlikable; to be undesirable

 싫어하다 / 싫어해요.
 [si-reo-ha-da]   [si-reo-hae-yo.]
= to hate; to not like

2) 예쁘다 / 예뻐요.
[ye-ppeu-da] [ye-ppeo-yo.]
= to be pretty; to be cute

 예뻐하다 / 예뻐해요.
 [ye-ppeo-ha-da] [ye-ppeo-hae-yo.]
= to consider someone pretty and treat them in such a manner

3) 슬프다 / 슬퍼요.
[seul-peu-da] [seul-peo-yo.]
= to be sad

 슬퍼하다 / 슬퍼해요.
 [seul-peo-ha-da] [seul-peo-hae-yo.]
= to feel sad and therefore express such emotions

In Korean, when you want to say "Don't be sad", "Don't do it", "Don't come", or "Don't go.", you use the construction "-지 마세요" after the verb stem. Since 슬프다, 예

쁘다, and 싫다 are not action verbs, you cannot use those verbs with "-지 마세요". You must to use the active verb form by adding "-하다".

Ex)

Don't be sad. = 슬퍼하지 마세요. (o) 슬프지 마세요. (x)

Don't hate me. = 싫어하지 마세요. (o) 싫지 마세요. (x)

Sample Sentences

1. 저는 우유를 좋아해요.
[jeo-neun u-yu-reul jo-a-hae-yo.]
= I like milk.

저는 우유를 안 좋아해요.
[jeo-neun u-yu-reul an jo-a-hae-yo.]
= I don't like milk.

2. 우유가 좋아요? 주스가 좋아요?
[u-yu-ga jo-a-yo? ju-seu-ga jo-a-yo?]
= Do you like milk? Or do you like juice?

3. 뭐가 제일 좋아요? = What is your favorite?
[mwo-ga je-il jo-a-yo?]

4. 뭐를 제일 좋아해요?
[mwo-reul je-il jo-a-hae-yo?]
= What do you like best?

* Here, another difference between 좋다 and 좋아하다 is that you can use 좋다 for the meaning of "to like" only about yourself, not about other people. If you want to say that Kyeong-eun likes Rain, you have to use the verb 좋아하다.

Ex) 경은 씨는 비를 좋아해요.
[gyeong-eun ssi-neun bi-reul jo-a-hae-yo.]

5. 저 좋아하세요?
[jeo jo-a-ha-se-yo?]
= Do you like me? Are you in love with me?

Sample dialogue

Track 44

A: 무슨 색깔 좋아해요?
[mu-seun saek-kkal jo-a-hae-yo?]

B: 빨간색이랑 노란색이요.
[ppal-gan-sae-gi-rang no-ran-sae-gi-yo.]

A: 파란색은 안 좋아해요?
[pa-ran-sae-geun an jo-a-hae-yo?]

B: 네, 안 좋아해요.
[ne, an jo-a-hae-yo.]

A: *What color do you like?*

B: *Red and yellow.*

A: *You don't like blue?*

B: *No, I don't like it.*

Exercises for Level 2 Lesson 22

1. "좋다" and "좋아하다" are similar in meaning but quite different in
[jo-ta]   [jo-a-ha-da]
usage. Which one is closer to "actively" liking something?

(   )

2. Use the verb "좋다" to write "I like the Korean language."
[jo-ta]

(   )

3. Use the verb "좋아하다" to say "I like the Korean language."
[jo-a-ha-da]

(   )

4. Using the verb "좋아하다", how do you say "민수 likes 2NE1."?
[jo-a-ha-da]

(   )

5. Using the verb "좋다", how do you say "What is your favorite?"
[jo-ta]

(   )

Check the
Answers on
p. 179

LESSON 23

만약, -(으)면

Track 45 After studying with this lesson, you will know how to say "if" in Korean. You will also be able to use it in context in your Korean sentences.

In order to express the meaning "if", you need to know two expressions: one is a noun, and one is a verb ending.

만약 = in case, if

-(으)면 = verb ending for "if"

In English, the word "if" is used at the beginning of a sentence to make the sentence conditional, but in Korean, you need to conjugate the verb as well. But don't worry, conjugation verbs in this manner is very easy to do.

How to conjugate verbs

In order to add the meaning "if" to a verb, you take the verb stem and add -(으)면 to the verb.

[-(eu)myeon]

1. Verb stems ending with a vowel + -면

   Ex) 자다 → 자면 (if you sleep)

2. Verb stems ending with ㄹ + -면

    Ex) 길다 → 길면 (if it's long)

3. Verb stems ending with consonants other than ㄹ + -으면

    Ex) 작다 → 작으면 (if it's small)

If you want to make you sentence clearer, you add the word **만약** [man-yak] in front of the verb or at the beginning of the phrase. Since most Korean sentences are heavily affected by verb endings toward the end of sentences, adding **만약** at the beginning makes it easier to understand that you are making the sentence conditional and saying "if".

Ex)

1)   Verb: **자다** = to sleep

    지금 자면 = if I sleep now
    만약 지금 자면 = if I sleep now

2)   Verb: **비가 오다** = to rain

    내일 밤에 비가 오면 = if it rains tomorrow night
    만약 내일 밤에 비가 오면 = if it rains tomorrow night

** In the second sentences for both of the examples, the listener can figure out that the sentence is going to be an "if" sentence just by hearing "**만약**".

If what you are saying is simple and the sentence is not very long, you don't always have to use the word **만약** in each sentence.

A little more conjugation practice for you:

먹다 = to eat
[meok-da]

먹으면 = if you eat it; if I eat it
[meo-geu-myeon]

** You can add the -았/었/였 suffix before -으면 to make a past-tense clause.

먹었어요 = I ate
[meo-geo-sseo-yo]
먹 + 었 + 으면 = if you ate it; if I ate it
[meo-geo-sseu-myeon]

사다 = to buy
[sa-da]
사면 = if you buy it; if I buy it; if they buy it
[sa-myeon]
샀다 = I bought
[sat-da]
샀으면 = if you bought it; if we bought it
[sa-sseu-myeon]

** You can even make it into the future tense by using -(으)ㄹ 거면.

보다 = to watch
[bo-da]
보면 = if you watch it; if I watch it
[bo-myeon]
봤다 = I watched
[bwat-da]
봤으면 = if I watched it; if they watched it
[bwa-sseu-myeon]
볼 거예요 = I am going to watch
[bol geo-ye-yo]
볼 거면 = if you are going to watch it
[bol geo-myeon]

Sample Sentences

1. 내일 비가 오면, 집에 있을 거예요.
[nae-il bi-ga o-myeon, ji-be i-sseul geo-ye-yo.]
= If it rains tomorrow, I'm going to be at home.

2. 이거 다 먹으면, 배가 아플 거예요.
[i-geo da meo-geu-myeon, bae-ga a-peul geo-ye-yo.]
= If you eat all of it, your stomach will hurt.

3. 리모콘을 찾으면, TV를 볼 수 있어요.
[ri-mo-ko-neul cha-jeu-myeon, ti-vi-reul bol su i-sseo-yo.]
= If you find the remote control, you can watch TV.

4. TTMIK에서 공부하면, 재미있어요.
[TTMIK-e-seo gong-bu-ha-myeon, jae-mi-i-sseo-yo.]
= If you study at TTMIK, it's fun.

5. 지금 안 오면, 후회할 거예요.
[ji-geum an o-myeon hu-hoe-hal geo-ye-yo.]
= If you don't come now, you will regret it.

This is not everything.

This is one of the most basic ways of making "if" sentences in Korean. There are other expressions you can use, such as "if only you had done it, I would have ...", but those will have to wait until we learn some other things first! In the meantime, enjoy practicing what you learned today!

Sample dialogue

Track 46

A: 저 내일 한강 갈 거예요.
[jeo nae-il han-gang gal geo-ye-yo.]

B: 만약 비 오면요?
[ma-nyak bi o-myeon-yo?]

A: 만약에 비 오면, 그냥 집에 있을 거예요.
[ma-nya-ge bi o-myeon, geu-nyang ji-be i-sseul geo-ye-yo.]

A: I am going to go to the Han River tomorrow.

B: What if it rains?

A: If it rains, I'll just stay at home.

Exercises for Level 2 Lesson 23

1. If "to sleep" is "자다" in Korean, how do you say "If I sleep now..."?

(   )

Match the Korean words with their English equivalents.

2. 보다
[bo-da]

3. 보면   a. if you are going to watch it
[bo-myeon]

4. 봤으면   b. if you watch it, if I watch it
[bwa-sseu-myeon]

5. 볼 거면   c. to watch
[bol geo-myeon]

                                      d. if I watched it, if they watched it

6. Write the following sentence in Korean: "If it rains tomorrow, I'm going to be at home."

(   )

Check the Answers on p. 179

LESSON 24

아직, 벌써

Track 47

In this lesson we are going to learn two new expressions that have opposite meanings.

아직 means "still" and "not yet".

In English, generally, the word "still" is used with positive sentences, and the word "yet" is more commonly used with negative sentences. However, in Korean, the word 아직 is used for both positive and negative sentences.
[a-jik]

아직 10시예요.
[a-jik yeol si ye yo.]
= It's still 10 o'clock.

아직 안 했어요.
[a-jik an hae-sseo-yo.]
= I haven't done it yet.

아직 아침이에요.
[a-jik a-chi-mi-e-yo.]
= It's still morning.

아직 몰라요.
[a-jik mol-la-yo.]
= I don't know yet.

To emphasize the meaning of "still happening" or "still not happening", you can add the particle -도 after 아직 to form 아직도. 아직도 has a meaning of criticizing the other person or being a little bit mad or angry.
[-do]

135

아직 몰라요?
[a-jik mol-la-yo?]
= You don't know yet?

아직도 몰라요?
[a-jik-do mol-la-yo?]
= You still don't know? How could you still not know?

아직 안 왔어요?
[a-jik an wa-sseo-yo?]
= He's not here yet?

아직도 안 왔어요?
[a-jik-do an wa-sseo-yo?]
= He's still not here yet?

네, 아직도 안 왔어요.
[ne, a-jik-do an wa-sseo-yo.]
= No, he's still not here.

벌써 means "already".

The usage of the word 벌써 is very similar to the English word "already". It's generally
[beol-sseo]
placed at the beginning of sentences, but it doesn't always have to be at the beginning.

It's already three o'clock.
= **벌써 세 시예요.**
[beol-sseo se si-ye-yo.]

It's three o'clock already!
= **세 시예요, 벌써!**
[se si-ye-yo, beol-sseo!]

Both of the sentences above work.

Sample sentences

벌써 왔어요?
[beol-sseo wa-sseo-yo?]
= Oh, you are already here!

벌써 끝났어요.
[beol-sseo kkeun-na-sseo-yo..]
= It's already over.

벌써 끝났어요?
[beol-sseo kkeun-na-sseo-yo?]
= Is it already over? Did it already finish?

이미 vs 벌써

Another word that you will often encounter when reading or listening to Korean that has the meaning of "already" is 이미.
[i mi]

이미 means "already" as well, so it seems asly 이미 and 벌써 have the same meaning, but in fact, Koreans often distinguish the meanings of these two words.

The difference between 이미 and 벌써 lies in whether you are already aware of a fact or not. When you and/or the speaker know about something already and talk about it, you use 이미. When you are just finding out about something as you speak, you use 벌써. People don't always stick to this rule, but this is the basic idea.

Ex)
그 사람은 이미 학교를 졸업했어요.
[geu sa-ram-eun i-mi hak-gyo-reul jo-reo-pae-sseo-yo.]
= He already graduated from school.

- You (and probably also the other person) have known about this fact since long before you say this sentence.

그 사람은 벌써 학교를 졸업했어요!
[geu sa-ram-eun beol-sseo hak-gyo-reul jo-reo-pae-sseo-yo!]
= He already graduated from school.

- You might have found out about this fact recently, or you already knew about this but the other person may have not known about it before you say it.

Because of this difference, in normal everyday situations where we find out about new facts or new information, Korean people use 벌써 more often.

벌써 비가 오고 있어요.
[beol-sseo bi-ga o-go i-sseo-yo.]
= It's already raining.

벌써 추워요.
[beol-sseo chu-wo-yo.]
= It's already cold.

벌써 끝났어요.
[beol-sseo kkeun-na-sseo-yo.]
= It's already over.

Sample dialogue

Track 48

A: 왜 일찍 왔어요?
[wae il-jjik wa-sseo-yo?]

B: 네? 지금 벌써 여섯 시예요.
[ne? ji-geum beol-sseo yeo-seot si-ye-yo.]

A: 벌써요? 몰랐어요.
[beol-sseo-yo? mol-la-sseo-yo.]

A: Why did you come so early?

B: What? It's already 6 o'clock now.

A: Already? I didn't know that.

Exercises for Level 2 Lesson 24

1. How do you say "still" or "not yet" in Korean?

(   )

2. How do you say "I don't know yet" in Korean?

(   )

3. "Already" is "벌써"". How do you say "Is it already over?/Did it already finish?"
[beol-sseo]

(   )

"이미" means "already" as well, so "이미" and "벌써" appear to have the same meaning, but in fact, Koreans often distinguish the meanings of these two words.

4. How do you say "He already graduated from school"? - You, and probably the other person, have known this information for a long time.

그 사람은 (   ) 학교를 졸업했어요.
[geu sa-ram-eun (   ) hak-gyo-reul jo-reop-hae-sseo-yo.]

5. How do you say "He already graduated from school"? - You may have found out this information just recently, or you already knew about this, but the other person may have not known about it prior to you telling him/her.

그 사람은 (   ) 학교를 졸업했어요! = How big is it?
[geu sa-ram-eun (   ) hak-gyo-reul jo-reop-hae-sseo-yo!]

Check the
Answers on
p. 179

LESSON 25

〰〰〰

누군가, 무언가, 어딘가, 언젠가

Track 49

In English, when you change the word "when" to "someday", "what" to "something", "who" to "someone", or "where" to "somewhere", the words change a lot in form. However, when you do this in Korean, there isn't much change to the original word except for an added ending.

In Korean, in order to change "when" to "someday", you just add -ㄴ가 (-n-ga) at the end of the word for "when", which is 언제. So 언제 becomes 언젠가.

The same rule applies to some other words.
누구 (who) - **누군가** (someone)
뭐 (what) - **뭔가** (= **무언가**) (something)
어디 (where) - **어딘가** (somewhere)
언제 (when) - **언젠가** (someday)

Sample Sentences

언젠가 미국에 가고 싶어요.
[eon-jen-ga mi-gu-ge ga-go si-peo-yo.]
= I want to go to the States someday.

언제 미국에 가고 싶어요?
[eon-je mi-gu-ge ga-go si-peo-yo?]
= When do you want to go to the States?

언젠가 일본에 갈 거예요.
[eon-jen-ga il-bo-ne gal geo-ye-yo.]
= I'm going to go to Japan one day.

언제 일본에 갈 거예요?
[eon-je il-bo-ne gal geo-ye-yo?]
= When are you going to go to Japan?

뭐 찾았어요?
[mwo cha-ja-sseo-yo?]
= What did you find?

뭔가 찾았어요?
[mwon-ga cha-ja-sseo-yo?]
= Did you find something?

뭔가 이상해요.
[mwon-ga i-sang-hae-yo.]
= Something is strange.

뭐가 이상해요?
[mwo-ga i-sang-hae-yo?]
= What is strange?

누구 만날 거예요?
[nu-gu man-nal geo-ye-yo?]
= Whom will you meet?

누군가 만날 거예요?
[nu-gun-ga man-nal geo-ye-yo?]
= Will you meet someone?

누군가 왔어요.
[nu-gun-ga wa-sseo-yo.]
= Someone came.

어디에 있어요?
[eo-di-e i-sseo-yo?]
= Where is it?

여기 어딘가에 있어요.
[yeo-gi eo-din-ga-e i-sseo-yo.]
= It is somewhere here.

BUT!!! (And this is important!) In Korean, like many other expressions, this rule is not always kept by everyone. What does this mean? It means that EVEN when you mean to say "someday", you can use 언제 instead of 언젠가, you can say 뭐 for "something",

어디 for "somewhere" and 누구 for "someone".

The distinction between 언제 and 언젠가 is stronger than the distinction between other words, but you can also replace 언젠가 with 언제 in many situations. When you use the original interrogative words instead of the -ㄴ가 form, you really need to pay attention to your intonation. The emphasis should be on the verbs, not the actual interrogative words themselves.

Sample Sentences

뭐 샀어요? (stress is on 뭐)
[mwo sa-sseo-yo?]
= What did you buy?

뭐 샀어요? (stress is on 샀어요)
[mwo sa-sseo-yo?]
= Did you buy something?

언제 중국에 갈 거예요? (stress is on 언제)
[eon-je jung-gu-ge gal geo-ye-yo?]
– When are you going to go to China?

언제 중국에 갈 거예요? (stress is on 갈 거예요?)
[eon-je jung-gu-ge gal geo-ye-yo?]
= Are you going to go to China someday/one of these days?

어디 가요? (stress is on 어디)
[eo-di ga-yo?]
= Where are you going?

어디 가요? (stress is on 가요?)
[eo-di ga-yo?]
= Are you going somewhere?

오늘 뭐 배웠어요? (stress is on 배웠어요?)
[o-neul mwo bae-wo-sseo-yo?]
= Did you learn something today?

오늘 뭐 배웠어요? (stress is on 뭐)
[o-neul mwo bae-wo-sseo-yo?]
= What did you learn today?

143

Sample dialogue

Track 50

A: 뭔가 이상해요.
[mwon-ga i-sang-hae-yo.]

B: 뭐가요?
[mwo-ga-yo?]

A: 화장이요.
[hwa-jang-i-yo.]

B: 아! 처음 해서 그래요.
[a! cheo-eum hae-seo geu-rae-yo.]

A: Something is strange.

B: What is strange?

A: Your makeup.

B: Ah! It's because I did it for the first time.

144

Exercises for Level 2 Lesson 25

1. If "when" is "**언제**", how do you say "someday" in Korean?
[eon-je]

( )

2. Since "what" is "**뭐**", how do you say "something" in Korean?
[mwo]

( )

3. How do you say "When are you going to go to Japan?"

( )

4. How do you say "I'm going to go to Japan one day"?

( )

5. How do you say "Something is strange"?

( )

Check the
Answers on
p. 179

LESSON 26

-(으)세요

Track 51   In this lesson we are looking at how to tell someone to do something by using polite Korean. This is one of the most essential things to be able to say, even when you are just asking for a favor.

In order to tell someone to do something, you add -(으)세요 to the end of the verb stem. Verb stems ending with a consonant are followed by -으세요 and verb stems ending with a vowel or with the consonant "ㄹ" are followed by -세요.

Ex)
시작하다 = to begin, to start
[si-ja-ka-da]
시작하 + -세요 = 시작하세요 = Please begin.
[si-ja-ka-se-yo]

오다 = to come
[o-da]
오 + -세요 = 오세요 = Please come.
[o-se-yo]

쉬다 = to rest
[swi-da]
쉬 + -세요 = 쉬세요 = Please get some rest.
[swi-se-yo]

고르다 = to choose, to pick
[go-reu-da]
고르 + -세요 = 고르세요 = Please choose.
[go-reu-se-yo]

접다 = to fold
[jeop-tta]
접 + -으세요 = 접으세요 = Please fold it.
[jeo-beu-se-yo]

Exception:

When a verb stem ends with the consonant ㄹ, you drop the ㄹ and add -세요.

팔다 = to sell
[pal-da]
팔 → 파 + 세요 = 파세요 = Please sell it.
　　　　　　[pa-se-yo]

We are introducing this verb ending, -(으)세요, as a way to tell someone to do some-
　　　　　　　　　　　　　　　　　[-(eu)se-yo]
thing, but this is one of the many variations where the honorific suffix -시 is used.
Within -세요, the suffix -시is included, but for now, please just focus on this particular
　　　　　　　　　　　　　　[-si]
usage of asking someone to do something.

Sample Sentences

1. 내일 세 시에 오세요.
[nae-il se si-e o-se-yo.]
= Please come here at three o'clock tomorrow.

2. 공부하세요!
[gong-bu-ha-se-yo!]
= Study! Do your studies!

3. 경은 씨, 빨리 일하세요.
[gyeong-eun ssi, ppal-li i-ra-se-yo.]
= 경은, hurry up and get some work done!

4. 경은 씨, 쉬세요.
[gyeong-eun ssi, swi-se-yo.]
= 경은, please get some rest.

5. 이거 저한테 파세요.
[i-geo, jeo-han-te pa-se-yo.]
= Please sell this to me.

6. 조심하세요.
[jo-si-ma-se-yo.]
= Be careful!

Some fixed expressions using -세요:

When you go into a store or a restaurant, the people who are working there will say to you,

1. 어서오세요.
[eo-seo-o-se-yo.]
= (lit. Come quickly) Welcome.

When someone is leaving, and you are staying, you say,

2. 안녕히 가세요.
[an-nyeong-hi ga-se-yo.]
= (lit. Go peacefully) Good-bye.

If you are the one who's leaving, and the other person is staying here, you say,

3. 안녕히 계세요.
[an-nyeong-hi gye-se-yo.]
= (lit. Stay peacefully) Good-bye.

How to say "Good night." in Korean:

4. 안녕히 주무세요.
[an-nyeong-hi ju-mu-se-yo.]
= (lit. Sleep peacefully) Good night.

Some words change their forms specifically for polite language, but we are going to introduce those words in our future lessons.

Sample dialogue

Track 52

A: 여기 앉으세요.
[yeo-gi an-jeu-se-yo.]

B: 괜찮아요. 금방 갈 거예요.
[gwaen-cha-na-yo. geum-bang gal geo-ye-yo.]

A: 그래도 앉으세요.
[geu-rae-do an-jeu-se-yo.]

B: 네. 감사합니다.
[ne. gam-sa-ham-ni-da.]

A: Please sit down here.

B: It's okay. I'll be leaving soon.

A: But you can still sit down.

B: Okay. Thank you.

Exercises for Level 2 Lesson 26

1. When you want to tell or ask someone to do something, you add the ending -
아/어/여세요 to the verb stem. How do you say "Do it"?
[-a/eo/yeo-se-yo]

(   )

2. "To rest" is "쉬다". How do you say "Get some rest"?
[shi-da]

(   )

3. "To be careful" is "조심하다". How do you say "Be careful!"?
[jo-sim-ha-da]

(   )

4. "To study" is "공부하다" and "doing something difficult" is described in Korean as
[gong-bu-ha-da]
doing it "열심히". How do you say "Study hard!"?
[yeol-sim-hi]

(   )

5. When you go into a shop or a restaurant, what will the people who are working
there say to you to mean "Welcome"?

(   )

Check the
Answers on
p. 180

-아/어/여 주세요

Track 53 In our previous lesson, we looked at how to tell someone to do something. This could be said in a nice or polite way, but when you want to be nicer and ask for a favor, there is another verb ending you can use.

Instead of just adding -(으)세요 after the verb stem, if you add -아/어/여 + 주세요, the sentences have the nuance of asking for a favor or asking the other person to do something "for you".

Ex)
오다 = to come
오세요. = Please come.
와 주세요. = Please do me a favor and come.

하다 = to do
하세요. = Do it.
해 주세요. = Please do me a favor and do it for me.

Changing -세요 to -아/어/여 주세요 does not only make the sentence more polite, but it also adds the meaning of "for me". Even if you are using the same verb and even if you don't literally say the words "for me (lit. 저를 위해서)" in Korean, just using -아/어/여 주세요 at the end will automatically make the sentence mean "do it for me, please."

LEVEL 2

TALK TO ME IN KOREAN

For example, if you just want to say "아이스크림 사세요" ("Buy some ice cream"), it can mean "buy yourself some ice cream" or "buy some ice cream for your friends", but in Korean, if you say "아이스크림 사 주세요" using the -아/어/여 주세요 form, you mean "Please buy me some ice cream", or if you are the one who's selling the ice cream, you could mean "Please buy some ice cream from me if you want to help me."

Often times, when you want to ask for help, it is more natural to add -아/어/여 주세요 at the end. For example, it's not very natural to say "저를 도우세요!" (from the irregular verb, 돕다, to help) when you mean "Help me!" You need to say "저를 도와 주세요" or just "도와 주세요" to sound more natural.

Let's look at some more examples of how -세요 and -아/어/여 주세요 can be used in contrast.

1. **가르치다** = to teach
   [ga-reu-chi-da]
   가르치세요. = Teach. / Please teach. (to whom is unknown)
   [ga-reu-chi-se-yo.]
   가르쳐 주세요. = Please teach me.
   [ga-reu-chyeo ju-se-yo.]
   경은 씨한테 가르쳐 주세요. = Please teach 경은 (how to do that).
   [gyeong-eun ssi-han-te ga-reu-chyeo ju-se-yo.]
   경은 씨한테 스페인어 가르쳐 주세요. = Please teach 경은 Spanish.
   [gyeong-eun ssi-han-te seu-pe-i-neo ga-reu-chyeo ju-se-yo.]
   스페인어 가르쳐 주세요. = Please teach me Spanish.
   [seu-pe-i-neo ga-reu-chyeo ju-se-yo.]

2. **보다** = to see
   [bo-da]
   보세요. = See it. / Please see it.
   [bo-se-yo.]
   봐 주세요. = Please see it, and I'd appreciate it. / Please be kind and see it.
   [bwa ju-se-yo.]
   이거 봐 주세요. = Please look at this
   [i-geo bwa ju-se-yo.]
   숙제 봐 주세요. = Please look at my homework.
   [suk-je bwa ju-se-yo.]

Now, if you've become somewhat familiar with the 주세요 ending, let us take a closer look at what 주세요 means.

주세요 comes from 주다, which means "to give", so by adding 주세요 after a verb, you add the meaning of "give me the act of" doing something, so it means "do it for me." And -아/어/여 is just a connecting part for make the pronunciation a little softer.

If you want to speak a little less formally, you can say 줘요 instead of 주세요. 줘요 is a little more casual than 주세요 and politer than just -세요.

Sample sentences

1. 영어를 배우고 있어요. 도와 주세요.
[yeong-eo-reul bae-u-go i-sseo-yo. do-wa ju-se-yo.]
= I'm learning English. Please help me.

2. 도와 줄 수 있어요?
[do-wa jul su i-sseo-yo?]
= Can you help me?

3. 배 고파요. 김밥 사 주세요.
[bae go-pa-yo. gim-bap sa ju-se-yo.]
= I'm hungry. Buy me some kimbap.

4. 무서워요. 같이 가 주세요.
[mu-seo-wo-yo. ga-chi ga ju-se-yo.]
= I'm scared. Please go with me.

Sample dialogue

Track 54

A: 더워요. 창문 열어 주세요.
[deo-wo-yo. chang-mun yeo-reo ju-se-yo.]

B: 창문이요?
[chang-mu-ni-yo?]

A: 네. 문도 열어 주세요.
[ne. mun-do yeo-reo ju-se-yo.]

B: 네, 알겠습니다.
[ne, al-ge-sseum-ni-da.]

A: It's hot. Please open the window.

B: Window?

A: Yes. Please open the door, as well.

B: Okay, I will.

Exercises for Level 2 Lesson 27

1. The expression that makes a sentence translate to "for me" or "do it for me" is -
아/어/여 주세요. How do you say "Do this for me, please"?
_[-a/eo/yeo ju-se-yo]

(   )

2. The verb for "to teach" is "가르치다". How do you say "Please teach me English" ?
_[ga-reu-chi-da]

(   )

3. The verb for "to buy" is "사다". How do you say "Please buy me that over there"?
_[sa-da]

(   )

4. How do you say "Please have a look at this"?

(   )

5. "Can you come with me?" is "같이 갈 수 있어요?".
How do you add the nuance of "Can you do me a favor and come with me?" to
the sentence?
_[ga-chi gal su i-sseo-yo?]

(   )

*Check the
Answers on
p. 180*

LESSON 28

-(으)로

Through our previous lessons we have learned a few particles to use in Korean, and in this lesson, we are learning another one! Yay! Let's look at the particle -(으)로.
_[-(eu)ro]

Construction:

Nouns ending with a consonant + -으로

Nouns ending in a vowel or the consonant "ㄹ" + -로

-(으)로 connects a noun and a verb very closely and can have various functions. -(으)로 can mark the ingredients that an object is made of, the cause of a disease or something that happened, the direction in which someone is going, or the status or identity of a person that is doing something. Let's look at some example below.

Ex)

1. **나무로 만들다**
[na-mu-ro man-deul-da]

= 나무 (wood) + -로 + 만들다 (to make)

= to make (something) with wood

Someone made this table with wood. = 누가 이 테이블을 나무로 만들었어요.

2. **왼쪽으로 가다**
[oen-jjo-geu-ro ga-da]

= 왼쪽 (left side) + -으로 + 가다 (to go)

= to go to the left

= to go through the left side

156

3. 이 길로 가다
[i gil-lo ga-da]

= 이 (this) 길 (street / road) + -로 + 가다 (to go)

= to go down this path

= to go down this road

4. 펜으로 쓰다
[pe-neu-ro sseu-da]

= 펜 (pen) + -으로 + 쓰다 (to write)

= to write with a pen

5. 한국어로 말하다
[han-gu-geo-ro ma-ra-da]

= 한국어 (Korean) + 로 + 말하다 (to speak / to talk)

= to speak in Korean

6. 치즈로 유명하다
[chi-jeu-ro yu-myeong-ha-da]

= 치즈 (cheese) + 로 + 유명하다 (to be famous)

= to be famous for cheese

7. 사고로 다치다
[sa-go-ro da-chi-da]

= 사고 (accident) + 로 + 다치다 (to get hurt)

= to get hurt in (from) an accident

By now, you may be able to identify a common factor in the various functions for 로 in all of the previous example sentences. By using -(으)로, we know that something is used as a channel, as a tool, as a device, or a method.

Sample Sentences

1. 이거 뭐로 만들었어요?
   [i-geo mwo-ro man-deu-reo-sseo-yo?]

   = What did you make this with?

   = What is this made of?

2. 오늘 택시로 왔어요?
   [o-neul taek-si-ro wa-sseo-yo?]
   = Did you come by taxi today?

3. 버스로 갈 거예요.
   [beo-seu-ro gal geo-ye-yo.]
   = I'm going to go by bus.

4. 저를 친구로 생각해요?
   [jeo-reul chin-gu-ro saeng-ga-kae-yo?]
   = Do you think of me as a friend?

5. 2번 출구로 나오세요.
   [i-beon chul-gu-ro na-o-se-yo.]
   = Come out through exit number 2.

6. 저는 TalkToMeInKorean으로 한국어 공부해요.
   [jeo-neun TalkToMeInKorean-eu-ro han-gu-geo gong-bu-hae-yo.]
   = I study Korean through TalkToMeInKorean.

Sample dialogue

Track 56

A: 이쪽으로 가는 거 맞아요?
[i-jjo-geu-ro ga-neun geo ma-ja-yo?]

B: 아니요. 저쪽으로 가야 돼요.
[a-ni-yo. jeo-jjo-geu-ro ga-ya dwae-yo.]

A: 아, 진짜요?
[a, jin-jja-yo?]

B: 네. 저쪽으로 가세요.
[ne. jeo-jjo-geu-ro ga-se-yo.]

A: Is this the right way to go?

B: No. You should go that way, over there.

A: Oh, really?

B: Yes. Please go that way.

Exercises for Level 2 Lesson 28

1. The word that indicates a method in which or an ingredient with which an object is made is "-으로" or "-로". When do you use "-으로" instead of "-로"?
   [eu-ro]   [ro]   [eu-ro]   [ro]

(   )

2. How do you say "with a pen"?

(   )

3. The word for "a chair" is "의자", and the word for "wood" is "나무". How do you say
   [eui-ja]   [na-mu]
"They made this chair of wood"?

(   )

4. How do you say "Please speak in Korean for me"?

(   )

5. How do you say "What did you make this with?"

(   )

Check the
Answers on
p. 180

LESSON 29

~~~~~~

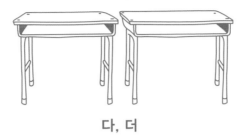

다, 더

Track 57   In this lesson, we are introducing how to say "all" in Korean.

다 = all, entirely, whole

And we will also review how to say "more".

더 = more

For many sentences where English speakers will use adjectives and nouns, Korean speakers use adverbs and verbs. This often becomes a challenge for translators and interpreters, but keeping this in mind will help you understand how to form more natural sentences in Korean.

Let's look at how 다 is used.
[da]

Ex)
1. 다 주세요.
[da ju-se-yo.]
= Give me all of it.

2. 우유 다 주세요.
[u-yu da ju-se-yo.]
= Give me all the milk.

3. 다 했어요.
[da hae-sseo-yo.]
= I've done all of it.

4. 다 왔어요?
[da wa-sseo-yo?]
= Are we there yet? (lit. Did we all come? / Did we come to all of it?)
= Did everyone come?

5. 다 살 거예요?
[da sal geo-ye-yo?]
= Are you going to buy all of it?

In some of the examples above, it looks as if the word 다 is working as a noun, and it is, but it has a stronger influence on the verbs so you can actually think of 다 as an adverb.

[da]

커피를 마시다
[keo-pi-reul ma-si-da]
= to drink coffee

커피를 다 마시다
[keo-pi-reul da ma-si-da]
= to drink all the coffee

In the second sentence above, the English word "all" was used to describe "the coffee", but in Korean, the word 다 was used to describe the action of drinking (마시다).

책을 읽다
[chae-geul ik-tta]
= to read a book

책을 다 읽다
[chae-geul da ik-tta]
= to read all of the book
= to finish reading the book

Q: Then how do you say "all of the book" or "the entire book", if the word 다 only modifies verbs?
A: You can use other words like 전체 or 전부. "The entire book" is 책 전체 or 책 전부, but this might not sound very natural when used out of proper context. In most cases, it's better to use 다.
[jeon-che] [jeon-bu]

Let's look at how 더 is used.
[deo]

Ex)

1. 더 주세요.
[deo ju-se-yo.]
= Please give me more.

2. 더 있어요.
[deo i-sseo-yo.]
= There is more.

3. 더 사고 싶어요.
[deo sa-go si-peo-yo.]
= I want to buy more.

4. 옷 더 사고 싶어요.
[ot deo sa-go si-peo-yo.]
= I want to buy more clothes.

5. 뭐가 더 좋아요?
[mwo-ga deo jo-a-yo?]
= Which is better?

The same explanation for 다 applies to the word 더 as well, especially when modifying verbs. Although it looks as if 더 is used as a noun here, it is not. When you say 더 사고 싶어요, the sentence is actually closer to saying "I want to do the "buying action" more", rather than "I want to buy more of something."

10분 기다려 주세요.
[sip-bun gi-da-ryeo ju-se-yo.]
= Please wait for ten minutes.

10분 더 기다려 주세요.
[sip-bun deo gi-da-ryeo ju-se-yo.]
= Please wait for ten more minutes.

In English, you say "ten more minutes" but in Korean, you literally say, "do the action of waiting for ten minutes + more".

If you want to review how to compare two things using -보다 and 더, please check out Level 2 Lesson 21.

Sample Sentences

1. 전화 다 했어요?
   [jeon-hwa da hae-sseo-yo?]
   = Did you finish talking on the phone?

   = Did you make all the phone calls?

   = Did everyone make a phone call?

2. 준비 다 했어요.
   [jun-bi da hae-sseo-yo.]
   = I did all the preparation.

   = I prepared everything.

   = I finished the preparation.

   = All of us are prepared.

3. 더 보여 주세요.
   [deo bo-yeo ju-se-yo.]
   = Show me more.

   = Show me more of it.

4. 더 공부하고 싶으면, TTMIK에 오세요.
   [deo gong-bu-ha-go si-peu-myeon, TTMIK-e o-seoyo.]
   = If you want to study more, come to TTMIK.

   = If you want to do more studying, come to TTMIK.

Sample dialogue

Track 58

A: 선생님, 숙제를 더 많이 내 주세요.
[seon-saeng-nim, suk-je-reul deo ma-ni nae ju-se-yo.]

B: 네? 정말요? 다 할 수 있어요?
[ne? jeong-mal-yo? da hal su i-sseo-yo?]

A: 네. 다 할 수 있어요.
[ne. da hal su i-sseo-yo.]

B: 네. 좋아요.
[ne. jo-a-yo.]

A: Teacher, give me more homework.

   B: What? Seriously? Can you do all of that?

A: Yes, I can do it all.

   B: Okay. Great.

Exercises for Level 2 Lesson 29

1. What is the word for "more" in Korean?

(   )

2. What is the word for "all" in Korean?

(   )

3. How do you say "Did you do all of it?" or "Did you finish doing it?"

(   )

4. How do you say "I did all my homework"?

(   )

5. How do you say "I want to buy more"?

(   )

6. How do you say "I want to buy all"?

(   )

Check the Answers on p. 180

LESSON 30

-지 마세요

Track 59

Through some of our previous lessons, we learned how to tell or ask someone to do something. In this lesson, we will look at how to tell someone not to do something or to stop doing something.

Since you already know how to use -(으)세요 to tell someone to do something, you just have to know one more verb here:

말다 = to quit doing, to not do, to stop doing
[mal-da]

When you use the -(으)세요 ending for this word, it becomes **마세요** but, when you
[ma-se-yo]
want to combine **마세요** with other verbs and say "don't do" something, you need to
add the suffix -**지** after the verb stem.
[-ji]

Verb stem + -**지 마세요**

Ex)
가지 마세요.
[ga-ji ma-se-yo.]
= Don't go.

아직 가지 마세요.
[a-jik ga-ji ma-se-yo.]
= Don't go yet.

하지 마세요.
[ha-ji ma-se-yo.]
= Don't do it.

= Drop it.

= Stop it.

= Forget about it.

사지 마세요.
[sa-ji ma-se-yo.]
= Don't buy it.

Sample Sentences.

만지지 마세요.
[man-ji-ji ma-se-yo.]
= Don't touch it.

웃지 마세요.
[ut-ji ma-se-yo.]
= Don't laugh.

걱정하지 마세요.
[geok-jeong-ha-ji ma-se-yo.]
= Don't worry.

경은 씨한테 말하지 마세요.
[gyeong-eun ssi-han-te ma-ra-ji ma-se-yo.]
= Please don't tell 경은 (about it).

아직 보내지 마세요. 아직 다 안 썼어요.
[a-jik bo-nae-ji ma-se-yo. a-jik da an sseo-sseo-yo.]
= Don't send it yet. I haven't finished writing it.

Sample dialogue

Track 60

A: 거기 앉지 마세요.
[geo-gi an-jji ma-se-yo.]

B: 왜요?
[wae-yo?]

A: 물이 있어요. 만지지 마세요.
[mu-ri i-sseo-yo. man-ji-ji ma-se-yo.]

B: 네, 알겠습니다.
[ne, al-ge-sseum-ni-da.]

A: Don't sit there.

B: Why not?

A: There is some water. Don't touch it.

B: Okay, I won't.

Exercises for Level 2 Lesson 30

1. The Korean word for "to quit doing/to not do/ to stop doing" is "말다". [mal-da]
How do you say "Don't do it"?

( )

2. "To buy" is "사다". How do you say "Don't buy it"?
[sa-da]

( )

3. The word for "not yet" or "yet" is "아직". How do you say "Don't do it
[a-jik]
yet"?

( )

4. The word for "to give up" is "포기하다". How do you say "Don't
[po-gi-ha-da]
give up"?

( )

5. "A lot" is "많이" and "too much" is "너무 많이". How do
[ma-ni]   [neo-mu ma-ni]
you say "Don't buy too much of it"?

( )

Check the
Answers on
p. 180

T-money is quite possibly the greatest invention to ever grace the streets of Seoul and surrounding Gyeonggi-do, and it'll be the best investment of your life to get one of these to carry around with you when you come here. T-money comes in all shapes and sizes, is rechargeable, and is useful in every means of public transportation that Seoul and Gyeonggi-do has to offer (hence the name "T-money").

So let's say that you've arrived in Korea and don't have T-money yet. How do you get it?

Luckily, you can purchase and re-fill T-money at all subway ticket booths. These automated machines are pretty nifty and we will be sure to cover this subject in a later post! You can also purchase and recharge T-money at almost every convenience store in Seoul. Most stores have a T-money logo in the window so you know for sure that you can purchase and re-charge there. There are even a few convenience stores at Incheon Airport on the arrival floor where you can do this so when you get to Seoul or Gyeonggi-do, you'll already have it. This saves you from being super awkward and basically wearing a sign on your forehead that says "I'm a tourist!" when you try to take a bus ride by paying with cash. Actually, it's not THAT awkward to pay with cash, but why pay with cash when you can get a discount by paying with T-money?!

on a bus

~~~~~~~~

Discount? Yeah, that's right! Everyone loves discounts, and T-money gives you 100W off the basic cash fare, which is essentially 1,150W for every 10km travelled. Since transportation cost in Seoul is figured by distance, the T-money card will gives you a discount on up to 4 transfers in the subways and buses when you need to.

You can get a regular T-money card for 2,500W, and other speciality cards, key chains, phone charms, etc... range from 5,000W to 25,000W. Different cards are sold at different locations, so check out this link to see all the different kinds of T-money and it's sold: http://www.t-money.co.kr/jsp/tpub/tint/buy_guide.jsp.

in a subway station

T-money is refundable, but you have to pay a 500W fee to get your money back. If your balance is under 20,000W, just take your T-money to a convenience store to receive the refund on the balance only; however, some convenience stores are unable to refund the money. If your balance is more than 20,000W, you have to take it to the T-money headquarters right outside of Seoul Station, Exit #8 to get your money back. Or, you can just keep the T-money and the money on it for the next time you come to Korea because it NEVER expires!!

If you won't be in Seoul for an extended amount of time and don't want to purchase a T-money card, another option is the Seoul City Pass. With this pass, you can ride subways and local buses in Seoul as well as subways in the surrounding Gyeonggi-do area. You can ride them all for up to 20 times per day without a limit on distance. With the Seoul City Pass, you can also ride 3 different routes (palace, downtown, and night view) of the Seoul City Tour Bus without limit. Currently the prices for the Seoul City Pass are:
1-day = 15,000W
2-days= 25,000W
3-days= 35,000W

You can purchase this pass at the following establishments:

· GS25, Family Mart, and MINISTOP convenience stores
  (located on the arrival floor of Incheon International Airport)
· Dongdaemun Tourist Information Office
· Gwanghwamun Tourist Information Office
· Itaewon Tourist Information Office
· Gimpo Airport Tourist Information Office
· Samilgyo Tourist Information Office
· Myeong-dong Tourist Information Office
· Namdaemun Tourist Information Office
· Jamsil Tourist Information Office.

The Seoul City Pass Plus Card is a pretty flippin' sweet deal if you're a tourist and plan to be in Seoul for a while. It's essentially a T-money card with the added benefits of a Seoul City Pass for only 3,000W plus the money you put on it to use for transportation. You can ride any bus or subway in Seoul until you run out of money and have to re-fill. You can also take any of the Seoul City Tour Bus routes at a 5% discount!! With your Seoul City Pass Plus Card, you also receive a booklet and discount coupons to use everywhere in Seoul. This pass also gets you discounts at 60+ participating stores that include res-

taurants, attractions, eyeglass shops, beauty stores, and many more! You get all of this great stuff for only 500W more than a regular T-money card. Um, yeah...totally awesome!

in a taxi

You can purchase and recharge the Seoul City Pass Plus Card at any of the convenience stores in Korea as well as 종묘 (Jongmyo) and any of the 4 major palaces (Gyeongbokgung Palace, Changdeokgung Palace, Changgyeong-gung Palace, and Deoksugung Palace). This card is also refundable, but there is a 500W convenience fee to get your money back.

So that's our introduction to T-money. We hope it provided you with some good information about paying for transportation in and around Seoul.

Written by Stephanie Morris

***

Before you close this book,
we'd like to tell you "congratulations" for finishing TTMIK Level 2!
Way to go, and we'll see you in Level 3!

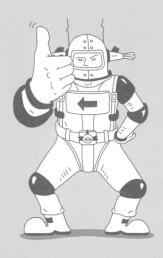

Answers

Leve 2 Lesson 1

1. 청바지 입을 거예요.
   [cheong-ba-ji i-beul geo-ye-yo.]
2. 뭐 팔 거예요?
   [mwo pal geo-ye-yo?]
3. 누구 만날 거예요?
   [nu-gu man-nal geo-ye-yo?]
4. 언제 점심 먹을 거예요? or
   [eon-je jeom-sim meo-geul geo-ye-yo?]
   점심 언제 먹을 거예요?
   [jeom-sim eon-je meo-geul geo-ye-yo?]
5. 내일 뭐 할 거예요?
   [nae-il mwo hal geo-ye-yo?]

Level 2 Lesson 2

1. (사과)를
   [reul]
2. (핸드폰)을
   [eul]
3. (공부)를
   [reul]
4. (시계)를
   [reul]
5. (여행)을
   [eul]

Level 2 Lesson 3

1. (책, 연필) 그리고 (공책)
   [geu-ri-go]
2. (저는 학생이에요.) 그래서 (돈이 없어요.)
   [geu-rae-seo]
3. (김밥은 맛있어요.) 그래서 (김밥을 자주
   [geu-rae-seo]
먹어요.)
4. (서울) 그리고 (부산)
   [geu-ri-go]
5. (아이유는 예뻐요.) 그리고 (노래도 잘해
   [geu-ri-go]
요.)

Level 2 Lesson 4

1. (친구)랑 / 하고 (영화 봤어요.)
   [rang] [ha-go]
2. (누구)랑 / 하고 (같이 갔어요?)
   [rang] [ha-go]
3. (김밥)이랑 / 하고 (라면 좋아해요.)
   [i-rang] [ha-go]
4. (동생)이랑 / 하고 (스케이트장 갈 거예요.)
   [i-rang] [ha-go]

5. (노트)랑 / 하고 (펜 가지고 오세요.)
   [rang] [ha-go]

Level 2 Lesson 5

1. 일요일 = b. Sunday
2. 화요일 = g. Tuesday
3. 토요일 = a. Saturday
4. 목요일 = c. Thursday
5. 수요일 = f. Wednesday
6. 월요일 = d. Monday
7. 금요일 = e. Friday

Level 2 Lesson 6

1. 그렇지만 / 그런데
   [geu-reo-chi-man / geu-reon-de]
2. 피곤해요. 그렇지만 / 그런데 괜찮아요.
   [pi-go-nae-yo. geu-reo-chi-man / geu-reon-de gwaen-cha-na-yo.]
3. 좋아요. 그렇지만 / 그런데 비싸요.
   [jo-a-yo. geu-reo-chi-man / geu-reon-de bi-ssa-yo.]
4. 어제는 비 왔어요. 그렇지만 /
   [eo-je-neun bi wa-sseo-yo. geu-reo-chi-man /
   그런데 지금은 비 안 와요.
   geu-reon-de ji-geu-meun bi an wa-yo.]
5. 어제 학교에 갔어요. 그렇지만 /
   [eo-je hak-gyo-e ga-sseo-yo. geu-reo-chi-man /
   그런데 일요일이었어요.
   geu-reon-de i-ryo-i-ri-eo-sseo-yo.]

Level 2 Lesson 7

1. 친구한테 / 친구한테서 받았어요.
   [chin-gu-han-te / chin-gu-han-te-seo ba-da-sseo-yo.]
2. 누구한테 물어봤어요?
   [nu-gu-han-te mu-reo-bwa-sseo-yo?]
3. 저한테 질문 있어요?
   [jeo-han-te jil-mun i-sseo-yo?]
4. 남자 친구한테 이거 줄 거예요. or
   [nam-ja chin-gu-han-te i-geo jul geo-ye-yo.]
   이거 남자 친구한테 줄 거예요.
   [i-geo nam-ja chin-gu-han-te jul geo-ye-yo.]
5. 친구한테 / 친구한테서 이거 얻었어요. or
   [chin-gu-han-te/chin-gu-han-te-seo i-geo eo-deo-sseo-yo.]
   이거 친구한테 / 친구한테서 얻었어요.
   [i-geo chin-gu-han-te/chin-gu-han-te-seo eo-deo-sseo-yo.]

Level 2 Lesson 8

1. 몇 시예요?
[myeot si-ye-yo?]
2. 세 시
[se si]
3. 한 시 십오 분
[han si si-bo bun]
4. 다섯 시 사십칠 분
[da-seot si sa-sip-chil bun]
5. 열 시 삼십 분 or 열 시 반
[yeol si sam-sip bun]   [yeol si ban]

Level 2 Lesson 9

1. 세 개
[se gae]
2. 다섯 명
[da-seot myeong]
3. 의자 세 개
[ui-ja se gae]
4. 몇 명 있어요? or 몇 사람 있어요?
[myeot myeong i-sseo-yo?] [myeot sa-ram i-sseo-yo?]
5. 두 명 있어요. or 두 사람 있어요.
[du myeong i-sseo-yo.] · [du sa-ram i-sseo-yo.]

Level 2 Lesson 10

1. 책 읽고 있어요.
[chaek il-kko i-sseo-yo.]
2. 뭐 하고 있어요?
[mwo ha-go i-sseo-yo?]
3. 뭐 하고 있었어요?
[mwo ha-go i-sseo-sseo-yo?]
4. 자고 있었어요.
[ja-go i-sseo-sseo-yo.]
5. 공부하고 있을 거예요.
[gong-bu-ha-go i-sseul geo-ye-yo.]

Leve 2 Lesson 11

1. 저는 학생이에요.
[jeo-neun hak-saeng-i-e-yo.]
2. 제 이름은 민수예요.
[je i-reu-meun min-su-ye-yo.]
3. 저는 20살이에요.
[jeo-neun seu-mu-sa-ri-e-yo.]
4. 저는 서울에 살아요.
[jeo-neun seo-u-re sa-ra-yo.]
5. 반갑습니다.
[ban-gap-seum-ni-da.]

Level 2 Lesson 12

1. 9월
[gu-wol]
2. 일
[il]

3. 9월 25일
[gu-wol i-si-bo-il]
4. 몇 월
[myeo-dwol]
5. 며칠
[myeo-chil]
6. 생일이 몇 월 며칠이에요?
[saeng-i-ri myeo-dwol myeo-chi-ri-e-yo?]

Level 2 Lesson 13

1. 저도 선생님이에요.
[jeo-do seon-saeng-ni-mi-e-yo.]
2. 한국어도 공부해요?
[han-gu-geo-do gong-bu-hae-yo?]
3. 오늘도 일해요?
[o-neul-do i-rae-yo?]
4. 물도 있어요:
[mul-do i-sseo-yo.]
5. 저도 이것 주세요. / 저 이것도 주세요.
[jeo-do i-geot ju-se-yo.]   [jeo i-geot-do ju-se-yo.]

Level 2 Lesson 14

1. 보기도 하다
[bo-gi-do ha-da]
2. 팔기도 하다
[pal-gi-do ha-da]
3. 저는 영어를 가르쳐요.
[jeo-neun yeong-eo-reul ga-reu-chyeo-yo.]
4. 저는 영어를 가르치기도 해요.
[jeo-neun yeong-eo-reul ga-reu-chi-gi-do hae-yo.]
5. 저는 수학을 가르치기도 해요.
[jeo-neun su-ha-geul ga-reu-chi-gi-do hae-yo.]

Level 2 Lesson 15

1. 만
[man]
2. 이것만
[i-geot-man]
3. 보기만 하다
[bo-gi-man ha-da]
4. 맥주만 마셔요.
[maek-ju-man ma-syeo-yo.]
5. 맥주만 주문했어요.
[maek-ju-man ju-mun-hae-sseo-yo.]

Level 2 Lesson 16

1. 조금 비싸요.
[jo-geum bi-ssa-yo.]
2. 아주 재미있어요.
[a-ju jae-mi-i-sseo-yo.]
3. 정말 이상해요.
[jeong-mal i-sang-hae-yo.]
4. 별로 안 비싸요.
[byeol-lo an bi-ssa-yo.]
5. 전혀 재미없어요.
[jeo-nyeo jae-mi-eop-sseo-yo.]

Level 2 Lesson 17

1. 갈 수 있어요.
[gal su i-sseo-yo.]
2. 할 수 없어요. / 못 해요.
[hal su eop-seo-yo.] [mot hae-yo.]
3. 이거 할 수 있어요?
[i-geo hal su i-sseo-yo?]
4. 지금 만날 수 있어요?
[ji-geum man-nal su i-sseo-yo?]
5. 수영할 수 있어요?
[su-yeong-hal su i-sseo-yo?]

Level 2 Lesson 18

1. 잘하다
[ja-ra-da]
2. 잘 못하다
[jal mo-ta-da]
3. 못하다
[mo-ta-da]
4. 저는 수영을 잘해요.
[jeo-neun su-yeong-eul ja-rae-yo.]
5. 저는 노래를 잘 못해요.
[jeo-neun no-rae-reul jal mo-tae-yo.]

Level 2 Lesson 19

1. 먹는 것
[meok-neun geot]
2. 가는 것
[ga-neun geot]
3. 책 읽는 것 좋아해요.
[chaek ilk-neun geot jo-a-hae-yo.]
4. 매운 것 안 좋아해요.
[mae-un geot an jo-a-hae-yo.]
5. 제 취미는 영화 보는 거예요.
[je chwi-mi-neun yeong-hwa bo-neun geo-ye-yo.]

Level 2 Lesson 20

1. Using 되다 is more common in colloquial situations.
2. 가야 돼요. / 가야 해요.
[ga-ya dwae-yo.] [ga-ya hae-yo.]
3. 써야 돼요. / 써야 해요.
[sseo-ya dwae-yo.] [sseo-ya hae-yo.]
4. 지금 해야 돼요.
[ji-geum hae-ya dwae-yo.]
5. 내일 어디 가야 돼요?
[nae-il eo-di ga-ya dwae-yo?]

Leve 2 Lesson 21

1. 더 빠르다
[deo ppa-reu-da]
2. 더 좋다
[deo jo-ta]
3. 커피는 물보다 더 비싸요.
[keo-pi-neun mul-bo-da deo bi-ssa-yo.]

4. 이 책은 저 책보다 더 재미있어요.
[i chae-geun jeo chaek-bo-da deo jae-mi-i-sseo-yo.]
5. 어제보다 더 일찍 왔어요.
[eo-je-bo-da deo il-jjik wa-sseo-yo.]

Level 2 Lesson 22

1. 좋아하다
[jo-a-ha-da]
2. 한국어 좋아요.
[han-gu-geo jo-a-yo.]
3. 한국어를 좋아해요. or 한국어 좋아해요.
[han-gu-geo-reul jo-a-hae-yo.] [han-gu-geo jo-ahae-yo.]
4. 민수 씨는 2NE1을 좋아해요.
[Min-su ssi-neun 2NE1-eul jo-a-hae-yo.]
5. 뭐가 제일 좋아요?
[mwo-ga je-il jo-a-yo?]

Level 2 Lesson 23

1. 만약 지금 자면
[man-yak ji-geum ja-myeon]
2. 보다 = c. to watch
[bo-da]
3. 보면 = b. if you watch it, if I watch it
[bo-myeon]
4. 봤으면 = d. if I watched it, if they watched it
[bwa-sseu-myeon]
5. 볼 거면 = a.if you are going to watch it
[bol geo-myeon]
6. 내일 비가 오면, 집에 있을 거예요.
[nae-il bi-ga o-myeon, ji-be i-sseul-geo-ye-yo.]

Level 2 Lesson 24

1. 아직
[a-jik]
2. 아직 몰라요.
[ə-jik mol-la-yo.]
3. 벌써 끝났어요?
[beol-sseo kkeun-na-sseo-yo?]
4. 이미   그 사람은 이미 학교를 졸업했어요.
[i-mi]   [geu sa-ra-meun i-mi hak-gyo-reul jo-reo-pae-sseo-yo.]
5. 벌써   그 사람은 벌써 학교를 졸업했어요!
[beol-sseo] [geu sa-ra-meun beol-sseo hak-gyo-reul jo-reo-pae-sseo-yo!]

Level 2 Lesson 25

1. 언젠가
[eon-jen-ga]
2. 뭔가
[mwon-ga]
3. 언제 일본에 갈 거예요?
[eon-je il-bon-e gal geo-ye-yo?]
4. 언젠가 일본에 갈 거예요.
[eon-jen-ga il-bon-e gal geo-ye-yo.]
5. 뭔가 이상해요.
[mwon-ga i-sang-hae-yo.]

Level 2 Lesson 26

1. 하세요
[ha-se-yo]
2. 쉬세요
[swi-se-yo]
3. 조심하세요!
[jo-si-ma-se-yo!]
4. 열심히 공부하세요!
[yeol-ssi-mi gong-bu-ha-se-yo!]
5. 어서오세요. (lit. Come quickly)
[eo-seo-o-se-yo.]

Level 2 Lesson 27

1. 이거 해 주세요.
[i-geo hae ju-se-yo.]
2. 영어 가르쳐 주세요.
[yeong-eo ga-reu-chyeo ju-se-yo.]
3. 저거 사 주세요.
[jeo-geo sa ju-se-yo.]
4. 이거 봐 주세요.
[i-geo bwa ju-se-yo.]
5. 같이 가 줄 수 있어요?
[ga-chi ga jul su i-sseo-yo?]

Level 2 Lesson 28

1. after the nouns ending with a consonant

2. 펜으로
[peo-neu-ro]
3. 이 의자는 나무로 만들었어요.
[i ui-ja-neun na-mu-ro man-deu-reo-sseo-yo.]
4. 한국어로 말해 주세요.
[han-gu-geo-ro mal-hae ju-seo-yo.]
5. 이거 뭐로 만들었어요?
[i-geo mwo-ro man-deu-reo-sseo-yo?]

Level 2 Lesson 29

1. 더
[deo]
2. 다
[da]
3. 다 했어요?
[da hae-sseo-yo?]
4. 숙제를 다 했어요.
[suk-je-reul da hae-sseo-yo.]
5. 더 사고 싶어요.
[deo sa-go si-peo-yo.]
6. 다 사고 싶어요.
[da sa-go si-peo-yo.]

Level 2 Lesson 30

1. 하지 마세요.
[ha-ji ma-se-yo.]
2. 사지 마세요.
[sa-ji ma-se-yo.]

3. 아직 하지 마세요.
[a-jik ha-ji ma-se-yo.]
4. 포기하지 마세요.
[po-gi-ha-ji ma-se-yo.]
5. 너무 많이 사지 마세요.
[neo-mu ma-ni sa-ji ma-se-yo.]

The CD on the next page contains key expressions, sample sentences, sample conversations and sample dialogues from the book.

You can download the MP3 files from the CD at http://TalkToMeInKorean.com as well.